MINI-WORK GARDENING

MINI-WORK GARDENING

Dr. W. E. Shewell-Cooper

Adam and Charles Black · London

First published 1976
Adam and Charles Black
35 Bedford Row, London WC1R 4JH

© W E Shewell-Cooper 1976

ISBN 0 7136 1623 7

Filmset and printed in Great Britain by
BAS Printers Limited, Wallop, Hampshire

By the same author

Contents

List of photographs

Preface

This book is the result of the experimental work I have been doing for the last twenty-five years. It started at Priors Hall, Thaxted, where my wife and I learned gardening the hard way, with spade, fork and hoe.

We had taught these traditional methods of gardening for years and we felt we had to find out for certain whether all this hard work was absolutely necessary. So we started to experiment with dug borders versus undug borders, forked borders versus unforked borders and so on and so forth, in our search for the truth.

In the end, after ten solid years of experiment and research, we felt we had the answers and we sold Priors Hall and bought Arkley Manor, where we could demonstrate what we had learnt. Thus, in 1960, we started off once more, and, with our elder son to help us, we have since then been demonstrating in the eight-acre gardens that it is possible – and indeed preferable – to garden productively without digging and forking, and that you can have a more beautiful garden, with better flavoured fruit and vegetables, using what is known as the compost mulching method.

Furthermore, because of the practice of putting the compost or sedge peat on top of the ground, there are no annual weeds at all. The curse of any garden is undoubtedly the groundsel, chickweed, shepherd's purse and the like. Every time you hoe, you bring thousands of weeds to the surface. They may have been lying below the top inch or so of soil for years, and by hoeing you yourself bring them to the surface where they germinate and grow quickly.

You can get rid of perennial weeds by using a substance like Weedol, which kills the chlorophyll in the leaves, or you can use what are called biological control methods for some weeds. Ground elder, however, can be controlled chemically, by sprinkling dry powdered sodium chlorate on the leaves of the plants, preferably in the spring.

So, you start without perennial weeds. Then by mulching with compost or using sedge peat you avoid annual weeds, and the scene is set for a beautiful garden with the minimum of effort and the minimum of labour.

If gardening is to be done on the mini-work plan, obviously there must be a new approach. New ideas should, of course, be introduced, but only when they have been fully tested and found to be successful. Someone must experiment, report, and be satisfied with results – and that is where *The Good Gardeners' Association* at Arkley plays an important part.

Arkley Manor is near Barnet and only twelve miles from Marble Arch. It can be visited, by appointment, by those who wish to see how what the author says actually works out in practice. The advice in this book comes from one who has for some thirty years been an avid experimenter, and who has now discovered, he believes, a simple and effective approach to the craft of gardening.

There is obviously no point in doing any job for the sake of it. Why mix dozens of different composts for pot plants when one will do? Why prune fruit trees hard when they bear far better if not cut about? Why dig two spits deep when better results can be obtained by very shallow forking and no digging at all? Why adopt formal hedges when informal hedges look better and do not need regular cutting? This book should have an appeal to all who are keen on the best of all hobbies, but in particular to those who are prepared to drop any old-fashioned pre-conceptions in their approach to gardens and gardening.

This book is, therefore, for those who want to enjoy their gardens and who don't mind being called lazy gardeners. It is a book for people who want to have their gardens looking tidy and beautiful with the minimum of work. It speaks of simplicity, it speaks of mechanization, and it emphasises, too, the importance of standardization.

I wish to thank Mrs Katherine Blackburn, Dip. Hort. (Swanley) for helping with the proofs, and Mr J Frank Milner for proof reading expertise plus general tidying up, and my thanks also, of course, go to Mrs Christine Ralph for typing the manuscript so patiently and carefully.

W E Shewell-Cooper

The Good Gardeners' Association
Arkley Manor
Arkley
Near Barnet, Hertfordshire

Dedicated to Mr A A G Black
who loves his Bonsai tree!

1 Introducing the minimum work garden

The minimum work garden is based on nature. When you go into the forest or woodland glade you may admire a beautiful oak spreading out its branches to the sun. It bears an enormous crop of acorns every year which animals, like squirrels and pigs love to eat. It has glorious green leaves born on strong sturdy branches, yet no one ever forks the ground under the branches. The surface is never hoed nor chemical fertilizer ever applied.

What happens then? The leaves of the autumn trees fall down and form a carpet. In addition the manure produced by birds, squirrels, rats, mice, roving deer, foxes and badgers is deposited on and among the leaves. The flies, wasps, bees, beetles, daddy-long-legs, and butterflies all drop their faeces on the leaves also. In addition, dead bodies may be deposited there – birds, wasps, flies, mice and so on. The carpet of leaves then becomes, as it were, nature's compost heap.

The worms, as part of their job, then pull into the soil the leaves, the dead flies, the feathers of the birds, the manure, etc. Thus they not only do the digging, for they can tunnel down to six feet, but they also see to it that the humus content of the soil is built up every year without man having to do anything about it.

It is the cheapest form of gardening. It is the easiest form of gardening – most important of all, it ensures that the healthiest plants are produced, and in the case of vegetables and fruits, those with the most delicious flavour. This is the basis for my method of mini-work gardening in fact.

The mini-work gardener then looks at nature and does everything possible to work *with* it. He ceases to have a passion for deep digging. He knows that the worms will do it for him and once he has left the soil alone, given the necessary organic matter, the population of worms will be built up in a comparatively short time (i.e. one million per each half acre garden).

He will buy sedge peat, if he hasn't got enough of his own compost to use as a top dressing, (or mulch) on his soil. His spade will only be used to make a hole to put in the trees, roses, shrubs or whatever other plants he wishes to grow. Once these permanent plants are in and the soil is well trodden down, a one-inch layer of dark brown powdery compost or sedge peat is put into position to prevent annual weeds.

The basis then of the mini-work garden is the layer of organic matter which is put *on top* of the soil and not forked in – except in the case of the vegetables where it can be deep raked in or in tiny gardens, hoed in.

No one need be ashamed of being a lazy gardener. The garden is there to be enjoyed. It should give a man, his wife and children a great deal of pleasure. For one person pleasure may consist in digging all day, and for another it could be lying in the sun in a deck-chair sipping a cooling drink and watching the roses blooming. The person however, who prefers working terribly hard and finds enjoyment in doing all things the difficult way is undoubtedly not one to read this book.

I have proved that it is possible to have a beautiful garden which gives pleasure to all, without a lot of work. But to achieve this there must be the right primary approach. The general garden planning may have to be altered. Some money may have to be spent in the process. A delightful, attractive, well-kept property with the barest amount of work should be the result.

There are some types of gardening which necessarily entail a tremendous amount of labour and these the mini-work gardener must forgo. Bedding out is an example. In this case there is a lot to do in autumn. Formal beds are planted with wallflowers, forget-me-nots or, say, winter flowering pansies, and when these have finished flowering in the spring, the beds must again be filled with dwarf dahlias, geraniums, or perhaps salvias. It isn't only the physical labour of bedding out that is exhausting, but it is the raising of plants in the greenhouse, the pricking out and the hardening off that makes the whole operation an expensive and tiring proposition.

There are those who must have a rockery. Because of its layout, because of the little pockets for the plants, mechanization is impossible. Hand work is the rule. Rock gardening is expensive in upkeep which is why you see few rock gardens today at the Royal Horticultural Show at Chelsea in the spring.

Similar remarks apply to the tall growing plants in the herbaceous border. Delphiniums are very beautiful but staking takes time and labour. As a member of the Delphinium Society I would never decry the growing of this beautiful flower but unfortunately it finds no place in this book for the minimum-work gardener. It is possible to have a beautiful flower border by sowing annuals, but think of the amount of time spent on soil preparation, sowing, thinning out, transplanting, watering and so on!

Remember these points when laying out a new garden or replanning an old one. Cast out all preconceived ideas of what a garden should be and be willing to sacrifice personal demands – if these demands mean forms of gardening which entail hard work. Go through this book chapter by chapter and learn the types of garden possible. Follow the methods advised and you will find it possible to have colour, scent, form and everything in fact that the keen horticulturist asks for.

It isn't only, however, the planning and layout, or the possible sacrifice of that pet plant. In addition the garden must be mechanized, and sometimes standardized, if work is to be reduced. Until recently, a friend of mine insisted on cutting his lawns by hand; because he had a lovely tennis court this became a burden. I persuaded him eventually to have an electric mower and he now cuts the lawns beautifully in a quarter of the time. Machines, therefore, should be seen as increasing the time available for really enjoying the garden.

Today Government horticultural advisers are telling commercial growers they cannot afford to water tomatoes by hand. It 'kills the job financially'. Some time ago a Scottish horticultural college proved that automatic trickle irrigation saved hours of labour and increased the crop of tomatoes by ten tons per acre. If the tomatoes sold for 10p a pound this meant an extra £1,140 per acre. Automation is a paying proposition for the market gardener, and for the amateur too.

It is important in any garden to consider introducing some automatic system of watering, in the greenhouse and out of doors. There is no virtue in the slavery of carting buckets of water about – it's easier to put the hose on to the tap and so guarantee that by means of a trickle 'harness' the plants get all the water they need automatically. They do, in fact, like it better that way.

It may be necessary to reduce the paths to a minimum, especially in the vegetable garden. It is easier to run such a garden when it is 'all in one piece'. All paths in the garden can in fact be improved by treating with one of the modern bitumistic substances then covering them with chippings before rolling. Ashphalt can be bought in bags and a 1 cwt bag of this substance will cover about 125 square feet. It should be applied cold to give a neat hard wearing surface and should be put on at an even thickness of three-quarters of an inch and then rolled firm. There is no need to wait for it to dry out as for instance with a concrete path. Just let it set and roll it.

In some gardens I have visited in an advisory capacity, the vegetable garden has been planted with apples, pears, plums and cherries, so that it is impossible to grow good fruit, because the trees cannot be sprayed regularly without ruining the vegetables, while it is equally impossible to grow good vegetables because the roots of the fruit trees rob the soil of much of its food. As a matter of fact, the necessary manuring of vegetables is quite different from that required for fruit trees, and fruit trees do better when grown in grass.

Where there are old fruit trees growing in a vegetable garden they will have to be scrapped and the owner will have to start anew as advised in Chapter 16.

Hedges must be kept to a minimum because they need cutting. Often it is advisable to put up a larch-lap fence. These fences are attractive and useful; they keep out the winds and retain your privacy. An alternative is the informal hedge described in Chapter 8.

Remember also that a lawn should be a lawn and not be cut up with little beds, each having to be planted up and edged carefully. Add top soil to any little beds you have right away and sow them with some good lawn-grass seed.

All the methods described have been tried out by the author. The experiments continue year after year and thus it is possible to keep up to date. The schemes advised in various chapters do work: they are not just imagined. There is no magic. It may be necessary to spend a fair amount of money for the first three months or so but in years to come the garden will bring you its reward. Forward then to a mini-work garden and an easier life.

2 No need for digging

As has been suggested seriously in Chapter 1 a mini-work garden is a no-digging garden. Mention gardening without digging and some people think of you as a crank. Land has been cultivated for generations. Farmers have ploughed from the earliest of days. How can seeds be sown unless the top soil is loose, so that they can be slightly buried, even though the earth may have to be firmed afterwards?

Consider this: good plants have in fact been grown for years without digging. The author has proved this in his own garden for at least twenty-five years. There are today many amateurs who garden without digging year after year, and get very good results, winning prizes at the local shows with their produce. Excellent crops can undoubtedly be grown without digging and the tens of thousands who have come to Arkley Manor, near Barnet, have seen this for themselves.

We have drawn attention to what happens to the leaves when they fall. This feeding done by nature comes from above, i.e. top dressings given in nature's way. In nature then, there is always this passing back into the soil that which was taken out by the roots.

This return to the earth of the organic matter it so badly needs makes it living soil. This is what is meant in Genesis III, 19, when God spoke to Adam and said 'In the sweat of thy face shalt thou eat bread till thou return unto the ground; for out of it wast thou taken; for humus thou art and unto humus thou shalt return.' This passing back of the body into the soil creates 'the complete circle'. The late Sir Albert Howard writing *Soil Fertility as the Basis of Public Health* said: 'It is the circulation of protein in nature that creates disease resistance and fertility and humus is the first step in bringing this about'.

It would seem that nature's plan is to return to the soil that which was taken out by means of an organic dressing. The worms then take over and do their tunnelling which is, in fact, 'the digging' of the mini-work gardener. The worms do the job instead of the fork and spade. By not digging the gardener, in fact, allows the worm population to increase and thus hundreds of worm 'casts' may easily be produced at the rate of at least fifteen tons per each one acre garden each year!

Because these worm casts are five times richer in nitrogen, seven times richer in phosphates, and eleven times richer in potash than ordinary soil, the 'growing power' of the soil will be tremendously increased, at no cost to the gardener at all. In addition, the tunnelling done by the worms ensures better drainage and allows easier movement of air in the earth. If the no-digger 'harnesses' his worms so to speak, he can get them to do the daily job of applying fertilizers in a simple manner.

Eighty per cent or more of the hard working good bacteria are found in the top 3 or 4 ins of the soil. Thus it is foolish to dig this in a spade's depth as most people do, and so completely upset (at any rate for the time being), their proper function in the earth. The 1 in top dressing given to the soil either by powdery compost or sedge peat, is exactly what is needed to help the work of the bacteria and the worms.

Most gardeners believe in rotting down all the vegetable refuse they can collect from the house and garden. (Simple composting methods are explained in Chapter 3.) Unfortunately, however, compost is normally dug in and not left as a top dressing. There is no argument as to its value – it is just a question of where it is to go. The digger says 'work it in' and the non-digger says 'put in on top'.

3 Natural feeding is simple

The minimum work gardener does not want to have to spend hours mixing various formulae of chemical fertilizers: one ounce of this, two ounces of that, three ounces of 'x' and so on. Some books would have the amateur make up six or seven or more different mixtures, one for fruit, another for flowers, a third for hard fruits, yet another for soft fruits and so on. Life is too short for such intricate preparations, nor are they necessary or advisable.

The expert leek grower may turn to his microcosmic salt for his exhibition specimen. The sweet-pea fan swears by his bullocks' blood for outstanding effectiveness. The maiden aunt may give her aspidistra a little milk, but for the mini-work gardener to enjoy his garden there must be some standardization, some organic fertilizer which will suit all crops and which will, in addition, be the perfect activator for the compost heap.

The most important step to take with regard to soil feeding is to make all the compost possible, and to make it properly. Use this either as a top dressing or cultivate it in. Where enough compost is not available, use additional sedge peat either as a top dressing or mulch, or fork it in to provide the organic matter needed in the top 2 in of soil. Then, having done everything possible to add humus to the ground, turn to organic fertilizers to help provide the extra plant foods required in a garden which is going to produce the best results.

It is always better to use organic fertilizers than chemical or what may be called completely inorganic fertilizers. First, the addition of some organic material helps to build up the humus content of the soil, whereas putting on pure chemicals may easily depress the content. Secondly, organics generally yield up their plant foods more slowly and over a long period, and thus for the normal garden they give better results.

Many of the biggest and most successful market gardeners use large quantities of organic fertilizers each year, and as good businessmen, they would not be paying the higher price for such fertilizers if they thought purely chemical ones would do as well.

The difference is that the mini-gardener with his organic manures plans to feed the helpful bacteria and so allow them to see to the feeding of the plants. The artificial fertilizer fanatic aims to try and feed the plants direct.

FISH OR SEAWEED MANURE

It is convenient to standardize the 'feeds' and use what is called a complete fertilizer (that is, one containing all the necessary plant foods) with an organic base. A good fish or seaweed manure is ideal, and both can now be bought almost entirely free from any objectionable odour. One is made from fish waste and fish residues, and without any additions it is naturally rich in nitrogen and phosphates and the other, of course, from natural seaweed. Manufacturers, however, usually add potash during the process of drying and packing.

The organic fertilizer (with low potash content) should be used all over the garden at about 3 ozs to the square yard. This is the standard dressing, and every spring the ground that is to grow crops should receive this feed. Sometimes a second application should be given in the early summer, either when another crop is being planted out, or in order to encourage some plants that may have been lagging behind. Where a fish fertilizer is bought with a low potash content, wood ashes can be used at 8 oz to the square yard. An organic fertilizer with a high potash content should be used for the plants that particularly need this food, for example, tomatoes, sweet-peas, roses, redcurrants and gooseberries.

A fertilizer of this kind is called a safe food. It can be applied along the rows of plants if they are growing, and lightly hoed or watered in. On the other hand, it can be given to the soil before the plants are put out, or applied prior to seed sowing.

For pot plants growing under glass a fertilizer with a ten per cent potash content is generally used. For those growing in small pots only a pinch of the feed is necessary, while for those in 8 or 9 inch pots, such as chrysanthemums, the usual advice is to apply as much as will go on a 5p piece, to make a similar application three weeks later, another three weeks after that and so on.

A fish or seaweed fertilizer can also be used as the activator for the compost heap, so that the gardener does not have to buy anything else.

LIQUID MANURES

The alternative to fish manure is a liquid like Farmura or McInnes seaweed manure. Gardening books have advised the use of liquid manures for years, but in the past it has been impossible to prescribe any dilution that would contain the right amount of plant foods. Liquid manures made from pure urine tend to be unbalanced, and therefore produce coarse, leafy plants. Urine is far better used on the compost heaps than diluted and applied direct to the soil.

The modern bottled liquid manures, however, are quite safe, and once again it is advisable to use two types – one that contains about eight per cent nitrogen, seven per cent phosphates and four per cent potash, and the other containing four per cent nitrogen, seven per cent phosphates and eight per cent potash. Concentrated liquid manures should be diluted with water in accordance with the maker's directions at the rate of two teaspoons per gallon. Plants that are very gross feeders may have double this strength. Take the teaspoon as being equal to $\frac{1}{8}$ oz and consider that the gallon contains 150 oz.

Some gardeners reading this may think that the amount of food given is too little, but it is better than the ordinary nutrient concentration found in any well fed garden soil.

The advantage of liquid feeding is that it is almost foolproof. Giving too much is merely temporary waste. Do not forget that the feeding roots of plants often stretch out four times further than the plants themselves, and so the liquid manure may be profitably applied quite a distance away.

I am sometimes asked how much liquid manure should be given: for a row of plants at least one pint of the diluted plant feed per foot, and for plants not in rows about one gallon per square yard. The exceptions are plants like runner beans, which, when growing 6 or 7 ft high, may easily need a gallon of food per foot row. It would be a waste of time and also unenjoyable gardening if doses had to be applied daily. Normally, in the autumn and spring, once a month is ample, in a hot summer and especially on dry soils once a week.

THE SECRET OF MAKING GOOD COMPOST

There is all the difference in the world between a proper compost heap and a rubbish heap. Unfortunately, thousands of people do not know this, with the result that they use the half-rotted material from a rubbish heap which can easily be full of weed seeds, diseases and pests. It is therefore extremely important to know:

1 What can be put onto the compost heap and
2 How a heap should be made and what activator to use. The whole point of an activator is that it helps to 'feed' the bacteria, the temperature of the heap will rise to 160–180° F. and kill the diseases, the pests and the weed seeds.

People have complained that a compost heap smells or that it produces flies; others have complained that it becomes a breeding place for rats or mice. The answer to all who complain in this way is that they haven't got a compost heap at all, but just a garden rubbish heap. This may easily smell because putrefaction can take place instead of the correct day-by-day regular rotting down.

There are, of course, those who won't be bothered – they would much rather burn their rubbish,

1 Because they enjoy making bonfires and
2 They say it produces good ashes which are as valuable as compost.

The bonfire-maker is the regular menace for it has recently been shown that the smoke in such fires may contain huge concentrations of cancer-producing benzypyrene.

If the vegetable waste is put into a dustbin then, of course, it costs the ratepayer more because of the necessary clearance by the local Council's workers. The writer is one of those who is anxious to save the ratepayers' money by introducing Municipal composting systems in every town and city. It is perfectly simple to compost garbage from dustbins either with some activator, such as fish manure, or with the sewage from towns and cities which is so often available in vast quantities.

The gardener's wooden bin In the normal garden it is best to make compost in a large wooden box or bin. The box is three-sided and has no bottom and no top, so the word bin is perhaps a better term. The size of it will vary in accordance with the size of the garden. For a large garden of, say, three acres or so it would be a good thing to have four bins, each one 10 ft by 10 ft and extending to a height of say 7 ft. When the first bin is full, the gardener – be he amateur or professional – should start filling up the second bin. Then, at the end of six months the compost in bin No. 1 should be ready for use and so this is made available again.

For gardens of half an acre, only two bins should be necessary. These should be about 4 ft by 4 ft and, say, 5 ft high. There must be a 1 or 2 inch space between the planks used to make the bin so as to provide adequate ventilation. It is most important that the floor should be ordinary soil because this gives the opportunity for the

worms to burrow their way up into the heap before the
heating-up time, and again, when the heap has cooled
down again. The worms can play a great part in making
good compost.

Some people like to cover the heap when it is completed
– with an inch or so layer of soil with the idea of keeping
the heat in. Others like to make a wooden cover and they
place this on top of the heap when it has reached the right
height. Yet another good alternative is a thick layer of a
woollen blanket or old carpet.

If the weather is very dry, as it is sometimes in the
summer, then it may be necessary to water the heap so
as to give the bacteria 'a drink' and so as to prevent the
vegetable waste from drying out. In countries like South
Africa and Australia it is best to have a pit and to 'build up'
the compost heap below ground. This helps to prevent
the vegetable waste from drying too quickly.

But whether the compost is in a heap or pit it is important never to allow it to become either sodden or too dry.

What can be put on the heap The motto of the good
composter should be 'Anything that has lived can live
again in another plant.' So, he can put on to his compost
heap the tops of the peas and beans, the potato haulm, the
yellowing leaves of the cabbages, sprouts, and the like, the
stumps of the cabbages and cauliflowers once they have
been bashed up with the back of an axe on a chopping-
block. Newspapers, if they have been soaked well first and
torn up, tea-leaves and coffee grounds; peelings like those
of apples, oranges and bananas; egg-shells; fish bones;
any woollen and cotton scraps; the dust from the vacuum
cleaner and, if you can get it, the hair from a barber's
shop. In addition of course, you can add the leaves from
the trees, weeds, lawn mowings, plus a certain amount of
sawdust, but do not put this on too thickly.

Be very careful *not* to put on the heap plastic, nylon,
cellophane, polythene, wax cartons, milk-bottle tops,
broken crockery and stones; the thick prunings from

apple trees and the like, nor the older branches of hedges and roses. All plastic and nylon products are synthetic and having never lived are useless on the compost heap.

Layer by layer The vegetable waste, whatever it may be, must be put on to the compost heap layer by layer. First of all a 6 inch layer of waste and then a sprinkling of the activator, another 6 inch layer of organic matter, another sprinkling of the activator; a third layer of waste, more activator, and so on right up the heap. I've sometimes described this as being like a sandwich cake where you get the sandwich part and then the jam, the sandwich, more jam, and so on. It is important that each layer should be kept absolutely level. It is necessary to ensure that the heat is engendered evenly right the way through the heap, and this can only be done when every time the vegetable waste is put on it is trodden down and kept absolutely level.

In the gardens of *The Good Gardeners' Association* at Arkley, the end posts of the bins have white markings up them every six inches and whichever gardener puts on the last lot of waste to reach one of these levels knows that he is the one to add the activator.

PLATE 1. The author levelling the garden waste in one of his compost bins before applying the activator.

Of course, at certain periods of the year, like late October and November (i.e. leaf fall in Great Britain), tremendous quantities of waste become available and it may be possible to put on several 6 inch layers in a day. In mid-summer, on the other hand when there may be only kitchen waste and a few weeds available, it may take the whole week before the 6 inch layer is reached. The general rule however, holds good. The activator is applied when the level is reached

Activators There are a number of activators which give good results. *The Good Gardeners' Association* uses dried poultry manure, seaweed manure, dried farm-yard manure or fish manure at about 3 oz to the square yard. It is possible to use pigeon manure or rabbit manure, dried blood, or even sewage sludge. It is definitely better to use natural organic manures, and never to do the composting with one of the advertised 'chemicals'. There are, however, seaweed activators which have given very good results, and where people are not too finicky human bedroom slops can be used with success.

Earlier on it has been said that the compost will be ready in six months. This does depend to a great extent on the weather. In the winter the composting always takes longer. A compost heap completed in October in Great Britain therefore may not be ready until May or June. It depends to a certain extent also whether the vegetable waste to be composted is soft. Lawn mowings, for example, will compost down far quicker than bashed-up cabbage stumps. In fact, it does help if the soft material can be intermingled whenever possible with the harder waste, for then the one helps to rot down the other.

When the browny-black powdery substance called 'compost' comes out of the bin at the end of the period it contains no weed seeds, no pests, no diseases. It is in the state, so to speak, just before it turns into humus and is quite ready to be converted into humus by the bacteria in the soil. It can either be forked in lightly into the top

PLATE 2. The author handles the powdery browny-black compost before it is applied to the ground as a top dressing.

2 in of soil or, better still, be put on top of the soil 1 in deep and left to allow the worms to pull in what they will.

It is also valuable because it contains vitamins, anti-biotics and enzymes and the micro-nutrients which are so important.

There is no permanently perfect soil. It's like a bank – put money in and you can get money out. The money in the soil is the humus – that wonderful bridge between life and death – so be sure to build up the humus content of the soil with compost and all will be well.

4 A good lawn with little work

There are very few gardens in Great Britain without a lawn. This is a good thing, for the British climate is ideal for lawn culture. On the whole it is the simplest and easiest form of gardening to manage. Most people spend very little time 'cultivating' their lawns. They just mow them, and if they have discouraged worms (because they don't like worm casts) they have in addition to carry out spiking.

The man who doesn't mind what type of plants he has growing in his lawn is quite happy to allow daisies, plantains and other weeds to abound. There is a very large garden in Yorkshire owned by a man whom the author has advised professionally. This wealthy 'Squire' loves the daisies in his lawn and says the little flowers always open to greet him in the morning. To such a man the use of hormones for killing lawn weeds is abhorrent.

Who is to say what type of lawn a man should have? It is for this reason that later in the chapter clover lawns are described, for these are ideal for chalky and limy soils. One can easily establish the old-fashioned chamomile lawn which is said to be the type that Drake played on when he had his bowls match just prior to the Armada. Vita Sackville-West showed me with great pride her thyme lawn, which never had to be cut. The little plants which made up the sward produced in the summer masses of little flowers much beloved by the bees.

The mini-work gardener must therefore decide what type of lawn or lawns he wishes to have. If it is the normal grass sward then he will see to it that it is mown regularly in the spring, summer and early autumn, by some mechanical means. The author is particularly fond of an electric mower because it is light and almost silent. One type is plugged from the house supply with a long flex and the other type has a battery which has to be charged from time to time. The former, working on a flex is perhaps the best for the normal-sized garden and the one with the battery for larger lawns.

The normal electric mower weighs about fifteen pounds and it is as simple to operate as a vacuum cleaner. With its high-speed blades, it shaves rather than mows and consequently passes back very fine cuttings to the sward. For this reason it can be used at certain times of the year without the grass box, and the fine cuttings fall back on to the lawn and help to increase its organic content. The motor runs at 8500 revolutions a minute and the normal width of an electric mower today is 1 ft. It is so light and moveable that it can be operated by quite young people. In the case of the one with the long flex, it is best to start near the house, and to work gradually to the other end of the lawn, paying out the flex as you go. If you work methodically from left to right in this way the flex does not get tangled or cut up by the blades.

With a battery-operated mower the charging of the cells can be done at home. A small trickle charger is used which is part of the machine and this can be attached to an electric point. The battery charges itself automatically during the night. This model is light and can be used by women with great success; it is easy to start and it propels itself.

The alternative is the petrol powered mower. It is simple to use and any amateur can work this mower nearly all day on only a gallon of petrol. A 4-stroke engine is very much quieter than a 2-stroke one. It has a starting handle any young person can operate and is not too heavy for a woman. There is a single lever which gives full command of the machine. When the lever is closed, the engine idles and the machine remains stationary. As the throttle is opened up the machine moves forward and does its job efficiently.

It is not difficult to set the knives. First you make certain the cutting cylinder is close to the bottom blade and then the screws can be adjusted on either side of the cutting unit. It is usual to adjust each screw separately and alternately. When set correctly, the knives should revolve freely and at the same time be able to cut a leaf on a piece of writing paper at the end of the bottom blade.

A motor mowing machine should not be used with the bottom blade pressing on the grass. If it does the cutters are likely to be damaged by the bottom blade being forced upwards. As a result the machine works heavily and the turf is badly mown. Keep the bottom blade just clear of the ground so that it does not press the grass down.

Here are two ways the gardener can save labour when mowing. The first is to remove the grass box when full and put the mowings as a mulch on the beds nearby. Do not however, put the mowings on deeper than half an inch because if you do the grass is apt to heat up and then the stems of the plants around which it is placed may be damaged.

The second method is to have a wheelbarrow in position at one point – preferably one with a pneumatic tyre or large ball tyre. Stop the motor each time the round is completed by the barrow and deposit the mowings. If you prefer to mow up and down and get these long vista-like markings on the lawn, you must move the barrow slightly as the mowings get farther away from it to save carrying the box too far.

Alternatively, in the spring, when the first cuts are made, and in mid-summer when the grass is short and dry, remove the box and allow the mowings to drop onto the lawn. Don't believe those who say it saves time and money only to mow the lawn once in three weeks. The longer you leave it the more work you give yourself. It pays to mow weekly and then there is the minimum of work.

You can save time and money if you never cut the grass of the lawn lower than $\frac{3}{4}$ inch. It is those who shave a sward down to $\frac{1}{2}$ inch or so who ask for trouble. In the first place this gives the weed seed a chance of reaching the soil where the grasses are growing – and so you get plantains and daisies establishing themselves – and secondly the closer you cut the lawn the more do the grasses grow.

Rotary grass cutters Those who do not mind not having that long path-like look produced by normal motor mowing can use a rotary grass cutter, and the Westwood 4-stroke Rotary allows the owner to set the height of the cut at seven different settings ranging from $\frac{3}{4}$ inch to $3\frac{1}{4}$ ins. The machine starts effortlessly by means of an automatic recoil starter. The machine is light and manoeuvrable. It has four wheels and may be bought to cover an 18 inch or a 21 inch strip.

Such a rotary grass cutter is excellent for keeping the sward down among fruit trees and bushes as described in Chapter 16. This machine cuts the grass easily and quickly with its propeller-like blade flying around parallel to the ground and the grass is left where it is for the worms to pull in.

Those who are worried about grass banks can use a special long-handled grass cutter by Tarpens. This can either be powered by means of a tiny little engine which is fixed to the top of the 6 ft handle or it can be plugged into some electrical point. Plate 3 shows this tool being used among soft fruit: with it, it is possible to cut the grass right up to the base of the blackcurrants or red-currants.

Weed control Those who wish to have a lawn consisting of grasses only should use one of the hormone weed killers which can be watered onto the lawn by means of a normal watering can or be applied by a special little machine fitted with a small tank and roller, which ensures that the hormone liquid is evenly distributed. The local chemist with a Horticultural Department can supply the special liquid hormones in bottles or tins. A special selective weed killer will kill all common lawn weeds including yarrow and clover.

With many weeds, particularly plantains, creeping buttercups, and cat's ear, one application will do. With

PLATE 3. Growing grass under blackcurrants saves work. Note the special Tarpen long-handled grass cutter, which has a little engine on the handle.

self-heal, crane's bill, hawk-weed, hawkbit, sorrel, daisy, dandelion and knap-weed – two applications are necessary at intervals of about ten days. With bird's foot trefoil, clover, pearl-wort, yarrow and chickweed three applications are desirable at weekly intervals. It sometimes takes two or three years to get rid of yarrow, pearl-wort and clover, three applications being made each year. With liquid hormones it is necessary to see that the spray does not drift onto nearby flower beds. It is necessary to do the work on a dry day, but for the best results, don't choose a period when the soil is over-dry.

With hormones it is unnecessary to dig the weeds out. They die in situ. Even on a weedy lawn all that is needed (once the offenders have been killed) is to rake the bare patches over lightly and six weeks later sow some good lawn seed and slightly rake this. The alternative is to buy the grass Agrostis stolonifera Z.103 in little two-inch cardboard pots and plant these in the bare patches. This is a special spreading grass which soon occupies the space

and yet grows low and minimizes the need for lawn mowing.

If grasses are not encouraged to grow quickly on the
spots recently occupied by the weeds there is little doubt
that more weeds will come to take their place.

On lawns where there are very few weeds, what is
known as spot killing is possible by using a special aerosol
filled with a hormone-type spray. All you have to do then
is to stand just over a weed, press down the knob of the
aerosol and a jet of the hormone will emerge and land
on the leaves of the plant that it is desired to kill.

Worms Worms are helpful creatures and they are useful
in lawns from the point of view of drainage. People
however who use lawns for games dislike the worm casts.
These, when mowing takes place, often squash flat and
form muddy patches on the lawn which makes it look
unsightly. If, therefore, worms are a nuisance to you and
the lawn, then eliminate them.

The best way of doing this is to use Mowrah Meal
applied at 3 oz to the square yard. This is not poisonous
to birds or animals but once applied and watered will
bring the worms up in hundreds. They can then be swept
up and put on the compost heap.

When the worms have been eliminated, the gardener
has to spike the lawn in order to provide the aeration
which the worms would have done gratis. A long tined
fork must be plunged into the lawn 9 in or so deep perpen-
dicularly. This will have to be done every 18 in or so all
over the lawn and is quite a laborious piece of work. The
alternative is to buy a spiking machine which is somewhat
expensive. Therefore my advice to lazy gardeners is to
allow the worms to have their own way.

THE CLOVER LAWN

Clover can provide a special lawn. I tried this first at
Thaxted in 1950 where the land was very alkaline. If the

clover is kept cut regularly the leaves become beautifully small and a perfect carpet is produced which keeps dark green all the year through. Some people were horrified when they saw the Thaxted clover lawn because they had the idea that it was meant to be a grass lawn, and that the clover had 'unfortunately' taken charge!

Clover is easy to look after, and if you happen to have a limy soil, there is no difficulty in getting it established and the clovers smother out weeds. Sow pedigree wild white clover at the rate of 1 oz to the square yard. Prepare the ground by raking level in order to produce a fine surface tilth adding medium grade sedge peat at the same time at one bucketful to the square yard. Those who have not got a limy soil but would like a clover lawn must apply carbonate of lime at $\frac{1}{2}$ lb to the square yard in addition to the sedge peat.

Lightly rake in the seed and roll lightly afterwards. If the weather is dry give a good watering as fine 'artificial rain', through an overhead sprinkler. A clover lawn is of no value for playing games on – but it is an attractive feature where the idea is to have an unusual lawn which is easy to manage.

A clover lawn is ideal for the mini-work gardener because it only has to be cut regularly. It is seldom infested with weeds. It is not attacked by diseases, as grasses can be, nor is there ever much trouble from pests. In the case of acid soils however, carbonate of lime will have to be applied each year at $\frac{1}{4}$ lb to the square yard.

A CHAMOMILE LAWN

The great advantage of the chamomile lawn is that it never goes brown even in the driest summer. The mini-work gardener therefore finds it a first class lawn to establish on dry sandy soil. This lawn plant which has survived to us from Tudor times is not only liked because of its colour but also because of its delightful fragrance. It takes no more mowing than an ordinary lawn and in my limited experience, considerably less. By the way, there are those who claim that a chamomile lawn, because it is a herb, is considerably healthier for children!

There are two ways of establishing a chamomile lawn. The first is by sowing the seed at not more than a $\frac{1}{4}$ oz to the square yard. You prepare the ground in the same way as you would for any lawn, and then sow the seed and rake it in. Some people save money by mixing the chamomile seed with about three times the quantity of a good lawn seed mixture.

The seed should be sown at $\frac{1}{4}$ oz to the square yard, and, as the chamomile spreads quickly it is argued that in a couple of years it will have smothered out the grass. That is in fact what happened to the main lawn at Buckingham Palace.

As chamomile seed is expensive, many people prefer to raise plants in a special seed bed. This should be in a sunny spot, and it helps if, before sowing the seed, sedge peat is added at a bucketful to the square yard and lime at a similar rate. Tread the ground well afterwards, and finally give one light raking to leave the surface fine

The seeds should be sown 6 ins apart with the drills $\frac{1}{2}$ inch deep. They should be sown very thinly and it will help if you mix the seed with about three times the quantity of sand or fine soil first. Rake over lightly to cover and then leave the plants where they are until they are about six months old; then plant them out at intervals of 3 in square. They will not take long to spread and when they are growing well, the first good mowing can be carried out. A light rolling will help after mowing, and even before. But roll at least a week before mowing.

Using a special chamomile strain Mrs Warwick Trevondan, Wadebridge, Cornwall, has produced a flowerless spreading chamomile plant which is excellent for producing a minimum-work lawn. Plants can be bought for planting into level prepared ground 6 in apart and rapid growth takes place in the spring and early summer so that it is not long before a complete chamomile sward has been produced. The ordinary chamomile produces flowers if left alone and so can be a nuisance, but this chamomile never flowers. It just spreads and spreads and produces a beautiful dark green lawn, with the minimum of effort. It merely has to be kept mown in the summer like an ordinary lawn.

It is said that this is the original non-flowering strain as used on Plymouth Hoe by Drake for his bowls playing. This is also the plant that produces the beautiful lawn at the rear of Buckingham Palace.

THE STOLONIFEROUS LAWN

The third lawn possibility is one made with Agrostis stolonifera Z.103. This is a very fine grass which has a tendency to stifle weeds and which succeeds on poor soils. It is frost and drought resisting and slow growing. It is only usually necessary to mow just once a month on small lawns established with this grass.

This grass is planted in March, April or May as a rule. The soil is cultivated to a depth of not more than 3 in and sedge peat is added at one or two gallon bucketfuls to the square yard. The plants which arrive in small paper pots are then planted with a trowel, pot and all, at intervals of 9 in. If the weather is dry these must be well watered.

The plants soon grow numerous runners along the ground and they interlace over the area. Small nodes appear along the length of the runners and it is from these that the roots and leaves grow. These nodes must be kept in contact with the earth so that the newly formed rootlets will strike downwards. Therefore, to encourage this, rollers should be used over the area the moment the runners are 6 ins long. Repeat rolling monthly until the lawn is established.

When the roots from the little nodes are established, vertical green blades of grass appear and as these thicken they will cover the runners and form a beautiful green lawn. When this happens the lawn is given its first mowing, with the blades of the mower set high. It is necessary to avoid at all cost cutting into the masses of runners below. After three to six months, according to the time of the year, the turf should be firmly established and few, if any, weeds will be able to penetrate the stoloniferous formation.

As the grass comes in pots the planting can be done all the year round, but the best times for planting are March, April, May, August and September. These special Agrostis stolonifera Z.103 pots may be obtained from the Hartspring Nuseries, 22, Alfred Terrace, Walton on Naze.

ROLL OUT THE LAWN

It is now possible to buy lawn by the roll and just lay it down like a carpet on level soil. It is known as Bravura turf and is made by the Netlon firm. The special lawn seed is sown in a controlled moisture-retaining rooting compound which is laid on a laminated base of Netton mesh

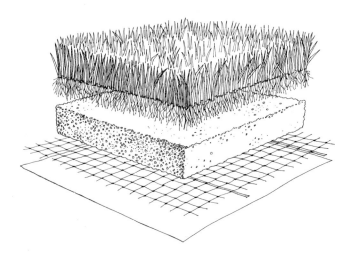

and polythene film, which protects the root structure and retains moisture before laying. The advantage of Bravura is that it can be laid in long strips. Just fork the soil over lightly, make it absolutely level and put down the lawn carpet – and, hey presto! you have a perfect lawn that has only to be treated in future as an ordinary sward.

PLATE 4. A roll of light-weight Netlon Bravura turf is very easy to handle.

Make simplicity the rule Let a lawn be a lawn: don't cut it up with lots of little flower beds of different types and sizes. It is when this happens that the gardener only makes work for himself. For there is a tremendous amount of edging to do. If there are to be flowers let them be along the edge of the lawn in one long sweep.

Edging the lawn automatically There is a good electric automatic lawn edger which works by means of a small battery. This is called Spin Trim. This long-handled little machine is merely pulled along the edges of the lawn which it cuts quickly and expeditiously. I have had one now for over seven years.

The Wolf Lawn Edge Trimmer This has a strongly constructed high quality steel frame, and contains a broad non-slip rubber roller with a star wheel cutter attached to one end. A twin-bladed self-sharpening stator blade is spring loaded against the star wheel cutter enabling either right- or left-handed operation. The tool head comes complete with Tap Right handle which needs no screws or other fitments yet may be removed for storage if required.

When it is pushed forward the self-sharpening and spring loaded blades cut over-hanging grass on lawn edges with a scissor action. The broad rubber roller enables easy guidance and balancing of the tool to be maintained even on undulating ground. The depth of the cut is approximately 1 inch.

PLATE 5. The Wolf Lawn Edge Trimmer.

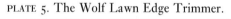

5 The flower border for the lazy man

The mini-work gardener will concentrate on flowering perennials that come up year after year and need the minimum of care and attention. Avoid bedding plants. Remember that when bedding out, first of all the plants have to be raised in the greenhouse, secondly, they have to be put out in the spring for flowering in the summer. Then, when they have finished blooming in the summer a new lot of bedding plants have to be put in, to make a show in the spring. The use of geraniums, salvias, antirrhinums, dwarf dahlias, wallflowers and forget-me-nots all make for a lot of work. Thus ordinary simple bedding, or even what is called 'carpet' bedding, has no place in this book.

The man who is going to enjoy his garden aims at having a wonderful show of flowers for as many months as possible without having the performance of raising the plants under glass, hardening them off in frames and planting them out. The aim is, as it were, for a permanent show.

The answer is the herbaceous border, a truly British concept. This method is hardly known in France or on the Continent. In England it has become fashionable as the result of the development of the erstwhile country cottage border. The problem of the herbaceous border (as may be seen in my book, *The Basic Book of the Herbaceous Border*), is the large number of plants that have to be supported by pea sticks and bamboos. There are the giant Michaelmas daisies which need lots of bushy pea sticks, or the stately delphiniums whose glorious blue spikes are often top-heavy and need the strengthening of a bamboo. There is nothing worse than tall spreading plants that fall over so that they become twisted, bent and ugly.

If time and labour must be saved by not supplying sup-
ports or doing any staking, then you must be careful only
to include specimens which are sturdy and will grow perfectly without support. Of course, it means that the
varieties of perennials will be limited but the lazy gardener
cannot have everything, and in the herbaceous border he
must sacrifice height to save labour.

A low border is apt to have a sameness about it, for one
of the joys of the perfectly planned herbaceous border is
the contrast between the tall spiky plants and the round
bushy ones. However in a low border which is easy to
run, much can be done to ensure that there is variety in
form and colour. One can design a border which will be
aglow from April to early October.

Plan carefully. It is worth using squared paper and
marking on a plan where the plants are to go. They must
be planted in drifts of four or five, not in a square or even
in lines. Put a little cross on the exact place for the plant
and mark a pencil outline round the five or six crosses
concerned, so as to mark the area to be devoted to each
variety.

At the paper plan stage these are some points to
remember:

1 Pinks should never be next to the bright crimsons.

2 Spiky-looking plants should be put next to bushy
ones if possible, the idea being to mix the shapes and
forms.

3 Place plants with little colour (those with greyish
foliage or creamy flowers) next to flowers with a pre-
dominant colour like the bright reds or glorious blues.

4 It may pay to keep a number of blues at the far end
of the border because these give the effect of distance.

5 It is a good thing to try and arrange that when one
drift of flowers fades, another is coming on.

6 Blues and mauves like contrast and it is good to have
them next to pale pinks and yellows, but stronger yellows
look best against bronzes and orange shades.

7 Maintain your planting in drifts of three or four plants and, in the case of wide borders, it may be wise to have six or seven plants in a group.

Of course it is no good planting perennials (which keep on growing year after year) unless the plot concerned is free from weeds like couch, ground elder, nettles, thistles and docks which are also perennials! Study Chapter 19, and be certain that you get rid of all perennial weeds before planting is done.

Make sure also that the plants will not starve and before planting take a fish or seaweed fertilizer applied at $\frac{1}{4}$ lb to the square yard and rake this in. The minimum-work gardener will not dig over the land before planting or even fork up farm-yard manure. He will merely make the necessary hole for the roots of the perennials which, when planted, must be trodden in well.

Sedge peat mulching
A top dressing of sedge peat or powdery compost must be given to the depth of an inch. If the weather is very dry, then at planting time it is better to soak the peat thoroughly first. The peat will smother the annual weed seeds and prevent them from growing. There will thus be no hoeing to do in the spring, summer or autumn. This dressing obviates the need for forking in the early winter. Worms will pull some of the peat or compost into the ground improving the soil so the plants will grow better.

Because of the activity of worms it is advisable to give another dressing in March or April the following year but this time a $\frac{1}{4}$ inch layer will usually only be necessary. Aim to plant the border in November, put on the first peat dressing the following May when the land has settled down and the second dressing, say, the following April. It is seldom necessary after this to use any more sedge peat except perhaps after ten years interval! This is a little exaggeration, but it does emphasise the fact that the mini-work gardener does *not* have to apply powdery compost or sedge peat *every year*.

This minimum-work herbaceous border can be left for five years and may not have to be disturbed for six years. After that the clumps will have grown large and it will pay to dig up the border in order to split the plants into smaller portions and replant, or to split up some of the largest plants. The outside portions of these clumps are reclaimed for replanting 'in situ' because they are younger and healthier and the central portions of the clumps are thrown onto the compost heap.

Never disturb a herbaceous border of this kind unless it is necessary. If the strong plants are kept cut back each spring so that they don't smother their neighbours, then, with scheming, it may be possible to leave the border down for eight years or more.

A newly planted border may look thin the first year but this does not matter. The thing is to give the herbaceous perennials plenty of room to grow and not to expect the border to be at its best the first season.

Think of the aspect when deciding where to have the border, for it is annoying to have all the flowers turning their heads towards the sun and away from the path down which the garden owner walks. Never have too narrow or short a border; for the medium-sized garden a border 6 ft wide is usual and for a very small garden 4 ft will do.

A little routine work Once the perennials have been planted and the sedge peat applied, routine work is very simple. A fish or seaweed fertilizer will be applied each March all over the top of the peat and allowed to work its way in naturally. In the autumn, the flowering stems will be cut to within 6 in of soil level, and when the leaves and the stems have been cleared they should be put onto a compost heap and sprinkled with the right activator.

No forking, no hoeing Your reward should be a beautiful flower border with little or no work, no hoeing, forking, or digging. In fact, using this method, the only labour is the cutting down of the stems in the autumn.

Some people even leave the tops on until the spring, so that during the winter the dead plants can provide shelter and food for the finches.

Suitable plants Following is a list of suitable plants which grow well with little attention. The height of the plants may vary slightly in different soil. A plant that may grow $4\frac{1}{2}$ ft wide on a good loam may only reach 3 ft on a poor, gravelly soil. The heights given are for an average soil. These plants should be obtainable from any good nurseryman and if there is any difficulty do not hesitate to consult me.

Name	Description	Height	Time of Flowering
Achillea Coronation Gold	A dwarf, gold flowered variety	$2\frac{1}{2}$–3 ft	July–October
Achillea Moonshine	Yellow-silver leaves	$2\frac{1}{4}$ ft	July–October
Achillea millefolium Cerise Queen	Bright and useful	$2\frac{1}{2}$ ft	June–August
Achillea taygetea	Primrose yellow; pale foliage	18 in	June–September
Aster (Michaelmas Daisy)			
Aster Alice Haslam	Rosy cerise	9 in	September–October
Aster Little Red Boy	Rosy red	14 in	September–October
Aster Margaret Rose	Lovely rose	1 ft	September–October
Aster Midget	Pale blue	1 ft	September–October
Aster amellus Brilliant	A lovely pink	$2\frac{1}{2}$ ft	September–October
Aster amellus Jubilee	Light lavender blue	20 in	September–October
Aster amellus Nocturne	Lavender blue	$2\frac{1}{2}$ ft	September–October
Aster ericoides Brimstone	Yellow starry flowers	$2\frac{1}{2}$ ft	October–November
Aster linosyris Gold Dust	Beautiful yellow – wiry	2 ft	October
Aster Novi-Belgii Alpenglow	Rosy red	2 ft	September–October
Aster Novi-Belgii Jenny	Intense Purple	18 in	September–October
Aster Novi-Belgii Gayborder Splendour	Dark cyclamen-rose	$2\frac{1}{2}$ ft	September–October
Aster Novi-Belgii Marie Ballard	Large double; light blue	3 ft	September–October
Aster Novi-Belgii Dandy	Purple-red flowers	12 in	September–October

Aster Novi-Belgii Royal Velvet	Gleaming violet flowers	2 ft	September–October
Aster Novi-Belgii Winston Churchill	Glowing ruby-red flowers	$2\frac{1}{2}$ ft	September–October
Campanula glomerata dahurica	Light violet	6 in	June–August
Campanula glomerata dahurica nana	Purple		June–August
Campanula glomerata dahurica Pixi	Violet-blue flowers	15 in	June–August
Campanula latifolia alba Brantwood	Violet-purple bells	$2\frac{1}{2}$ ft	June–July
Campanula persicifolia Pride of Exmouth	Dark blue, double	$2\frac{1}{2}$ ft	June–July
Catananche caerulea	Bears beautiful blue flowers	2 ft	June–July
Centaurea montana Violetta	Lavender-purple flowers	2 ft	May–June
Chelone barbata obliqua	Bears head of purple-red flowers	2 ft	August–September
Cynoglossum nervosum	Deep blue	18 in	June–August
Delphinium Belladonna-varieties			
Delphinium Blue Bees	Clear light blue	$3\frac{1}{2}$ ft	June–August
Dianthus Prichards variety	Pink; strong stems almost double	6 in	June–July
Dicentra eximia	Bears pale purple flowers	1 ft	May–September
Dicentra formosa	Dangling rose-red firs	18 in	April–June
Dictamnus fraxinella	Lilac-rose flowers; erect growth	2 ft	June–July
Doronicum plantagineum Miss Mason	Very free flowering yellow	2 ft	April–June

Name	Description	Height	Time of Flowering
Echinops ritro Veitch's Dwarf Blue	Steely-blue flowers	2 ft	July–August
Erigeron Darkest of All	Very deep violet-blue flowers	2 ft	June–August
Erigeron Rose Triumph	Lighter pink than Foerster's Liebling	2 ft	June–August
Geum borisii Dolly North	Deep flame orange	2 ft	June–July
Geum borisii Fire Opal	Intense Flame, semi-double	18 in	May–August
Geum borisii Mrs. J. Bradshaw	Semi-double brilliant scarlet	2 ft	May–August
Geum borisii rosii	Golden flowers	18 in	April–May
Helenium Coppelia	Warm coppery-orange	3 ft	July–August
Helenium Mme. Canivet	Clear yellow	2½ ft	June–August
Helenium Mahogany	Gold and brown red	2 ft	July–August
Heuchera Coral Cloud	Coral-Red flowers	2 ft	May–July
Heuchera Damask	Small glowing carmine-rose flowers	18 in	May–July
Heuchera Pretty Polly	Bright pink flowers	2 ft	May–July
Heuchera Oakington Jewel	Deep coral-rose with coppery tinge	2½ ft	May–July
Heuchera Sunset	Bears deep, fiery-red flowers	18 in	May–July
Heuchera Sparkler	Carmine and scarlet; dark green foliage	2 ft	May–July
Hosta fortunei	Lilac-blue flowers; glaucus leaves	2½ ft	July–September
Hosta lancifolia	Green leaves; lilac flowers	18 in	July–September
Hosta plantaginea grandiflora	White flowered, scented	2 ft	July–September
Hosta sieboldiana coerulea	Attractive foliage; pale lilac flowers	2 ft	July–September

Hosta Thos. Hogg	Large white-edged leaves	2 ft	July–September
Hosta incarvillea delavayi	Deep pink, early summer	18 in	May–July
Kniphofia atlanta	Yellow and red	2½ ft	July–August
Kniphofia macowanii	Slender spikes of orange red	2 ft	September–October
Kniphofia nelsonii major	Deep orange flame	2½ ft	August–September
Kniphofia tubergenii	Light yellow, neat and free	2½ ft	June–August
Kniphofia galpenii Bressingham Comet	Orange	20 in	September–October
Kniphofia galpenii Bressingham Torch	Flame Orange	2 ft	September–October
Liatris callilepsis	Intense lilac flowers	3 ft	June–August
Lythrum salicaria Brightness	Likes moist soil, spikes of bright rose	1 ft	July–September
Myosotis rupicola	Mountain forget-me-not	16 in	July–September
Nepeta Blue Beauty	Spikes of light blue flowers	2 ft	June–September
Nepeta mussinii	The lavender cat mint	1 ft	June–September
Oenothera cinaeus	Outstanding bright coloured foliage in spring; golden flowers	15 in	June–August
Physostegia Summer Spire	Pink flowers, erect strong spikes	2 ft	June–August
Pinks (see also Dianthus)	There are some double pinks that may be grown in a border without staking, i.e.		
Gloriosa	A double rose, scented		May–July

Name	Description	Height	Time of Flowering
Pinks cont.			
Mrs. Pilkinton	A stout-stemmed scented pink		May–July
Ipswich White	A glistening white		May–July
Poterium obtusum	Pink bottle brush spikes	$2\frac{1}{2}$ ft	July–September
Potentilla Gibson's Scarlet	Attractive	18 in	June–August
Ranunculus bulbosus speciosus plenus	Double yellow buttercup	9 in	May–June
Rudbeckia sullivantii Goldsturm	Deep yellow, black centre	$2\frac{1}{2}$ ft	July–September
Salvia hispanica	Purple; grey bushes	2 ft	July–September
Salvia superba East Friesland	A dwarf form	18 in	July–September
Solidago Cloth of Gold	Strong and free	18 in	July–September
Solidago lemora primrosa	Yellow trusses; very compact	2 ft	August–October
Statice incana rosea	Everlasting rose-coloured flowers	18 in	August–October
Thalictrum adiantifolium	Fern-like foliage; tiny white flowers	18 in	June–July
Tradescantia virginiana Iris	Blue flowers; showy	18 in	June–August
Trollius Canary Bird	Large pale yellow	2 ft	May–June
Trollius Wargrave Variety	Orange-yellow double flowers	1 ft	June–July
Verbena venosa	Violet-purple flower	18 in	July–August
Veronica Bowles' Hybrid	Shrubby growth; pink spikes	15 in	June–September
Veronica incana	Violet-blue flowers; silvery leaves	1 ft	June–August

Veronica spicata Barenrolle	Rich rose pink; deep green foliage	18 in	June–August
Zauschneria californica canescans	Red flowers, grey foliage	18 in	August–October

NB It pays to consult a good nurseryman about herbaceous plants and it could be that he may be able to suggest other species and varieties which would be suitable for a no-work border.

6 Flowers in the garden

SPLASHES OF COLOUR

The minimum-work gardener sometimes finds it possible to allocate various beds in his garden to one definite group of plants. These beds should be large enough to make a good splash of colour. Small circular beds in a lawn only make for extra work in both mowing and edging. A bed should be planned, say, with a fence as a background and the edging could be the green plastic strip which can be put down to conform to the outlines of whatever bed it is proposed to make. A bed between the wall and the path leading to the front door is one that is often suitable.

After planting, these beds are always mulched with sedge peat or brown powdery home-made compost, an inch deep so that there is no more forking, hoeing or raking to be done. An organic fertilizer like fish or seaweed manure is generally given at 3 to 4 oz to the square yard each February among the plants, but not on them. This is allowed to wash in naturally through the compost or peat. When and where worms have pulled in a fair quantity of the peat in order to build up the soil structure, an application of a further top dressing of compost or sedge peat, say $\frac{1}{4}$ inch deep may be necessary the following season.

It pays to start with clean soil, that is soil from which all perennial weeds have been eliminated. As has been advised in Chapter 19, strong hormone weed-killers may be used to get rid of docks, thistles, coltsfoot, perennial nettles and the like. Those who have taken over new gardens, or who are new to gardening, must realize that it is better to wait say a year in order to 'start clean', than to attempt to plant the first season with traces of perennial weeds present everywhere. No matter how carefully one forks out the roots of such perennials as bindweed and docks, little pieces are invariably left behind, which start the trouble all over again. Thus the use of a strong hormone like S.B.K. to eliminate perennial weeds has proved very useful.

Take note that there are special hormones like Dalapon or Dowpon for couch grass which is not killed by the strongest of the other types of weed-killers used say for docks, ground elder and the like. Take the advice of a local horticultural chemist.

EASY-TO-GROW CHRYSANTHEMUMS: KOREANS AND POMPONS

When chrysanthemums are mentioned to most people, they think of the huge blooms one sees in the shops or the rather tatty flowers found growing in suburban gardens late in the autumn. The minimum-work gardener will, however, concentrate on the dwarf-flowering miniature chrysanthemums, which will live happily in any part of the country.

It should be possible with them to ensure a succession of bloom from late July until late November in the south, from early August to October in the north. In fact even in the north the plants may be left out in the soil all the year, and frost and snow will not damage them.

Chrysanthemums will grow in almost any kind of soil. In very sandy soils it pays to fork really well-rotted compost (when preparing the bed) at the rate of two bucketfuls to the square yard and add, at the same time, if possible, wood ashes at half a pound to the square yard.

The plants are sturdy and should not need staking – they flower normally and no disbudding is necessary. They produce their side growths naturally, so there is no stopping or pinching back to do as with normal chrysanthemums.

After flowering, the plants are cut back to within one inch of soil level so that the bed is then tidy in the winter.

Planting out It is not advisable to plant until the soil has lost its stickiness in the spring. This usually means delaying planting until mid-April in the south and the end of April or early May in the north. Do not plant during heavy rains or in cold winds. See that the plants in their boxes and pots are well watered the day before planting.

Make a hole with a trowel sufficiently large to take the ball of soil and roots and insert this ball so that the plant will be growing in the same depth of soil as it was in the box or pot. Plant firmly and use the handle of the trowel to press the soil all round the roots. Then give the bed a really good soaking of water and a day later apply a top dressing of powdery compost or medium-grade sedge peat all over the ground an inch deep.

A month later the plants may have a short length of twiggy pea stick pushed into the soil at their backs. The idea is to give a little support and the branches will grow among the more woody branches of the pea sticks and so hide them.

As soon as the flower buds are seen, feeding may commence. Liquid seaweed should be given once a fortnight, dissolved in water, according to the instructions on the label. Given good weather, the chrysanthemums may remain in flower for ten or twelve weeks. The later varieties stay in flower almost to the end of the year. Immediately after flowering, the plants may be cut back hard and the roots left in the ground for another year.

The types There are two main types of chrysanthemums suitable for this minimum-work method culture. They are the Koreans – particularly the Cushion types – and the Pompons, and the bulk of the varieties grown will not be taller than 1 ft.

Koreans It is important to plant the varieties which grow no taller than 15 in or so. There are single, semi-double and double kinds and they are usually larger than the Lilliputs. They differ from Pompons in that the blooms are flat and about the size of a 10p piece.

Some of the blooms have quilled petals – the singles generally have broad petals while a few have blooms of a rosette formation. As will be seen from the descriptions given, some varieties bloom in August, others in September and October. It is worth while giving plants protection with square cloches like Access, in order to have flowers to cut in November.

List of Koreans

Name	Height	Blooming	Description
Ada Miles	18 in	August	Cream with yellow eye centre
Apricot Roach	18 in	Aug–Sept	Delicate apricot double
Autumn	15 in	Aug–Sept	Anemone centred red
Belinda	15 in	August	Golden amber single
Blush	18 in	September	Salmon pink double
Bubbles	16 in	August	Chestnut Bronze
Caroline	15 in	August	Vivid orange, globular
Copper Nob	2 ft	September	Copper colour, double
DonRaynor	2 ft	Sept–Oct	Dark pink, double.
Evenlight	15 in	September	Cerise Pink, semi-double
Fairy Rose	18 in	Aug–Sept	Pink single, yellow eye
Falgate	18 in	September	Light bronze, double
Gloria	15 in	Sept–Oct	Silvery pink, salmon centre
Herald	18 in	Aug–Sept	Light red-bronze, double
Janice Bailey	18 in	Aug–Sept	Rose-pink, almost double
Jewel	15 in	September	Pink salmon and red
Lemon Tench	1 ft	August	Lemon, single
Mulberry	15 in	Sept–Oct	Mulberry red, double
Russet Gem	15 in	September	Russet terra-cotta
Startler	2½ ft	Sept–Oct	Claret pink, semi-double
Wendy Tench	1 ft	September	Salmon pink, sturdy single

Pompons Though there are types of Pompons which grow to a height of 4 ft, we are concerned in this book with the varieties which grow no taller than 15 ins. It is possible to have Pompons in flower from the end of August until well on into October and the roundness and firmness of the blooms makes them most attractive.

If they are planted out firmly 18 ins apart they should grow perfectly without any attention at all.

List of Pompons

Name	Height	Blooming	Description
Alla	18 in	September	Bronze, deeper centre
Anartasin	2 ft		Rich wine, double
Amber Roach	18 in		Delicate amber
Billy Boy	1 ft		Golden-yellow
Blondie	15 in		Orangey-bronze
Bunty	18 in		Blush white, bronze centre
Cameao	15 in	Sept–Oct	White, solid blooms
Chick	1 ft	September	Bright pinky-bronze
Danny	18 in		Lilac-pink, flushed yellow
Denise	1 ft		Large golden flower
Dave Miles	18 in		Pink with salmon centre
Dick Raynor	2 ft		Orange with golden centre
Everley	18 in		Lilac-pink
Farie	12 in		Strawberry pink
Gaynor	18 in	September	Lovely yellow – strong
Gold Tit	18 in		Bright gold, red centre
Imp	18 in		Rich crimson
Jante Wells	15 in		Golden yellow
Joy	2 ft		Pale lemon yellow
Kim	15 in	Sept–Oct	Bronzy scarlet
Lassie	15 in	September	Medium pink, button like

Name	Height	Blooming	Description
Lottie	2 ft	Late Aug–Sept	Red with bronze tint
Mimi	1 ft	Aug–Sept	Red-bronze
Mosquito	18 in	September	Yellow – a perfect pom
Primrose Bouquet	1 ft	Aug–Sept	Primrose yellow.
Purple Fairie	15 in		Deep purple
Sherrie Saunter	2 ft	September	Light bronze
Tiptoe	1 ft		Brilliant gold
Tiara	18 in		Autumn bronze
Woking Profusion	15 in	Sept–Oct	Glowing yellow

THE PRIMULA BORDER

When the word primulas is mentioned most keen gardeners immediately think of a rock garden, but in fact there are many varieties and species which grow too large for such a garden. These are better planted in a large bed on their own. Incidentally, few people can afford a proper rock garden these days! It is the most expensive type of gardening there is.

Nevertheless, in a shadier part of the garden in which it might not normally be possible to grow a great variety of flowering plants there may be developed a primula garden. It was Colonel J. H. Stitt of Drumcairn, Blairgowrie who originally gave me the idea, so now we have at Arkley Manor a bed some 30 ft long and 5 ft wide in the centre, planted with many different varieties of primulas in bold groups of a dozen or more.

The border in which these primulas are growing is on the shady side of a good lilac hedge. Before planting, the soil was very lightly forked and really well-rotted old powdery compost was worked in at the rate of two bucketfuls to the square yard. The border was made wide enough to give sufficient space for the natural development of the plants. Bold planting was done, each drift being of one distinct species or variety. Species which flower at different times of the year were planted near one another so that the flowering of the one drift would cover up the non-flowering of another.

Each drift was well labelled, then the bed was covered with sedge peat to the depth of an inch. Home-made powdery brown compost will, of course, do instead. Since the time of planting nine years ago no hoeing or forking has been done, but it has been necessary, about once every six months to do a little bit of hand-weeding because as very few weed seeds – usually those of the *Poa annua* (the annual Meadowgrass) – blow onto the bed, they germinate quickly. Once established, primulas in a bed like this need little or no attention for four or five years.

Occasionally there are decayed leaves to be removed because these are attacked by aphids. Sometimes it is necessary to puff a little derris on to the plants to control the primula greenfly which attacks the plants often towards the end of the season, but that is all. At the end of five years some of the primula plants will have grown into large clumps and these will need splitting up into three or four for replanting Some of these split plants will of course be thrown away or given to friends.

There are a number of different species and varieties which can be grown, but the following are particularly easy, in addition to being beautiful.

List of Primulas

Name	Description	Height
Primula asthore	Apricot to mauve shades, candelabra	2 ft
P. bulleyana	Deep orange candelabra, July	2 ft
P. capitata	Attractive violet shaped flowers	$1\frac{1}{2}$ ft
P. denticulata	Lilac balls, April flowering	
Prichard's Ruby	Good red form	1 ft

Name	Description	Height
P. florindae	Tall, rounded leaves, huge heads of scented flowers, yellow and orange brown.	$2\frac{1}{2}$ ft
P. florindae waltoni	Very charming cross with pink flowers, June.	3 ft
P. involucrata	Creamy white flowers, conspicuous yellow eye.	1 ft
P. japonica Miller's Crimson	Intense colour, candelabra, June	18 in
P. japonica Postford White	Striking white variety	
P. pulverulenta Bartley strain	Shell-pink form with coloured eye	18 in
P. rosea delight (Visser de Geer)	Deep rose-red flowers	6 in
P. sieboldii alba	Outstanding white flower, May–July	18 in
P. vialii	Tall, 6-inch Red Hot Poker of scarlet bracts	1 ft
P. wilsonii	Dark purple candelabra	2 ft

SMOTHER PLANTS

The idea of the well-planned smother bed is that the plants that are used spread and spread and so cover the ground. The weeds cannot grow and there is no hoeing to do. A smother border is ideal for a bank that is difficult to cultivate or mow. The bed is planted up say in October or November with herbaceous and shrubby perennials which will grow evenly all over the ground. There may also be the bed which is rather awkward because it is in a semi-shady place where plants are not easy to grow.

Preparation Prepare the border making certain to eliminate all the perennial weeds. Where there is couch or scutch grass present in the soil use the weed-killer known as Dowpon or Dalapon, in accordance with the manufacturer's instructions. Where the weed ground elder is rampant, dry powdered sodium chlorate must be sprinkled on the leaves of the plants to destroy them. For other weeds like thistles and docks there is a strong hormone killer known as S.B.K.

It is of course useless to plant a smother border until all the perennial weeds have been eliminated. Once these are out of the way and the smother plants get going they will control annual weeds.

The border may be very lightly forked if it is lumpy, adding at the same time well-rotted compost at one bucket-ful to the square yard. (Gardeners who do not have their own compost use sedge peat at a similar rate.) You will need to apply a fish or seaweed fertilizer also at 4 ozs to the square yard and those who have wood ashes may use this as well at $\frac{1}{2}$ lb to the square yard also. Some form of potash is necessary when the border is shady, for potash can be regarded as 'artificial sunshine'.

The border will normally need a good treading, but where the soil is light and sandy a roller may be used to make certain that the soil is really firm. Now comes the planting.

PLATE 6. The smother border at Arkley Manor.

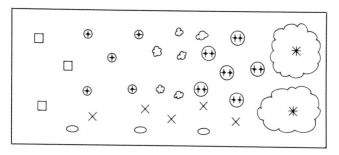

⊕   Vinca minor

⊕⊕   Vinca major

☁   Hypericum calicynum

□   Genista hispanica

✕   Heathers

◯   Hedera helix palmata

✳   Juniper horizontalis

Planting However large the border, be sure to buy sufficient plants for each drift to be planted up. In the case of wide spreading specimens like *Cotoneaster horizontalis*, each shrub will cover a three foot square area. The heathers will cover one square foot eventually – the Vincas need about eighteen inches on either side of them. The plants trail along the ground. They can if preferred be trained along the front of the border as well.

The plan as used at Arkley Manor can be reduced for a small garden or blown up where it is desired to smother a larger area. It is only necessary to increase or decrease the number of plants in the marked out drifts on the plan.

Having lightly forked over the area of lumpy soil, or by just raking the soil if fairly smooth – make holes for the smother plants that are going to be put in. Spread out the roots in the hole, cover with soil and tread down firmly. Complete the planting in accordance with the plan.

Then, if the weather is droughty and the soil dry, put a sprinkler on the end of a hose and by turning on the tap give the border artificial rain for at least three quarters of an hour. The plants must be well watered in. During the following few days continue the watering until the plants are 'settled in'.

It is after the soaking that the compost or sedge peat can be applied all over the ground one inch deep. This will not only prevent the annual weeds from growing but will conserve the moisture that has been given to the soil.

The border at Arkley Manor has proved extremely satisfactory and has given a great amount of pleasure to the thousands who visit the gardens month by month, a living demonstration that such a smother border really means a minimum of work. The main characteristic of each one of the plants included in this border is its ability to spread out over the soil and provide such a mat of leaves and flowers that no weeds can possibly grow.

Below will be found a description of some plants that are suitable for this border. Note the times of flowering, the colours of the blooms and the approximate height to which the plants will grow.

Name	Description
Berberis candidula	This bears bright yellow flowers in the summer followed by purple fruits in the autumn. It is an evergreen and never grows higher than about 2 ft.
Chaenomeles simonii	Low growing deep crimson flowers.
Cotoneaster horizontalis	Grows as flat bush no higher than 3 ft. The branches grow something like curved fish bones. Little white flowers are produced in the summer followed by bright berries in the autumn and winter.
Erica darleyensis	A beautiful heather and a rapid spreader.
Erica mediterranea	Winter-flowering until Easter; unaffected severest weather; very hardy.

Name	Description
Erica Springwood Pink	One of the dwarf spreading heathers, very free flowering; usually at its best in February, March and April; never grows higher than 6 in and bears dainty pink bells.
Erica Springwood White	Similar to Springwood Pink but producing masses of large white flowers during the first four months of the year. Both these are carnea types and therefore they will grow in soils containing lime.
Eunonymous radicans variegata	A beautiful Japanese plant which bears silver, golden and mauvey coloured leaves; never grows higher than about 1 ft; it can be kept cut back to about 6 in and looks attractive all through the year.
Genista hispanica	The true Spanish Broom; it produces fragrant yellow flowers from May–July; never grows higher than 2 ft, the shrubs growing like rounded balls.
Genista Lydia	Arching branches covered with yellow flowers in June.
Hedera helix palmata	A relation of the Common Ivy but one of the improved types which spread all over the ground. The leaves are five-lobed. The lobes are triangular and the plant spreads evenly all over the ground.
Helianthemum Honeymoon	Apricot flowers – deep green foliage.
Helianthemum oblongatus	Yellow and prostrate.
Hypericum calicynum	The true Rose of Sharon; height 15 in; yellow flowers.
Hypericum moserianum	The best dwarf form of the St. John's Wort; produces magnificent golden yellow flowers from July–October and never grows higher than 18 in, an extremely useful member for the shrubby border.
Juniperus horizontalis glauca	A blue-green form of the creeping Juniper. It is prostrate in growth and covers 5 ft, growing only 1 ft high off the ground.

Name	Description
Pachysandra terminalis	A hardy evergreen which loves a moist soil and shade; produces white flowers in the month of May and never grows taller than about 1 ft. There is a variety, Variegata, whose leaves are bordered and variegated with white.
Potentilla (Jackman's variety)	Produces a continuous display of brilliant yellow flowers all summer; should not grow higher than 2 ft and can be kept cut back; looks at its best in August and September.
Vinca major	This is the hardy evergreen periwinkle with largish blue flowers which are at their best from May to October. The plants never grow higher than 2 ft and trail over the ground.
Vinca minor	This is the lesser periwinkle. It produces much smaller leaves and blue flowers also throughout the summer. Like Vinca Major it trails over the ground and is an efficient weed smotherer. Can be had in many colours.

7 Shrubs without slavery

In the past shrubs could only be planted at certain seasons of the year, and invariably a garden owner would forget to do the planting at the right time, and thus have to wait a year or so before getting the job done. Today shrubs can be planted at almost any time when they are grown in containers. Most garden centres sell flowering shrubs of all kinds in tins or whalehide containers – and it is a simple matter to knock out the ball of soil containing the roots and plant firmly but shallowly. Some garden centres have special tools for cutting down the sides of the metal containers so that the shrubs can more easily be got out for planting.

Thus the mini-work gardener can plant at any time he wishes and can in addition have a flowering border which will ensure little or no work in the years to come. Flowering shrub gardens are very popular and fashionable now and rightly, for such plants do not need spraying like fruit bushes, do not need digging up every four or five years like herbaceous perennials and hardly need any feeding at all.

Once carefully planted in accordance with some plan the border will go on looking beautiful year after year almost unaided. There are shrubs bearing beautiful blossoms in the spring, shrubs which look lovely all through the summer, and shrubs which have glorious berries in the autumn, while others have fascinating autumnal tinged foliage in October and November. There are even shrubs which flower in mid-winter such as *Viburnumtinus*, *Prunus subhirtella autumnalis* and *Hamamelis mollis*. A flowering shrub border can indeed be a thing of joy and beauty for almost every month of the year – and with minimum work too.

Flowering shrubs have been called the rich man's fancy and the poor man's necessity! This is because of the low maintenance costs. The only advantage perhaps of wealth is that the very best plants can be bought at the start instead of having to add to the border as funds allow.

Don't aim at buying something unusual or difficult for rareness' sake. The flowering shrub border is not meant to be a museum, but something that will be gay and colourful for most months of the year. It is designed, remember, not to require hoeing, pruning, staking, or external replanting.

The activities of cats, dogs or even children should not unduly disturb a well planned shrub border. Never be disappointed because the border doesn't look at its best for the first few years. It is always possible to throw a few annual flower seeds into the soil in between the shrubs the first year or so and rake them in to add some colour in the first seasons. If the shrubs are planted from containers, they will look attractive right from the beginning, but of course it takes three or four years for the border to look its best.

Don't overplant with too many shrubs in order to hide blank spaces. Your idea may be to remove every other shrub in four year's time but you will never do so! The results of such crowding will merely be an overgrown mess – and a tragedy. Be patient and save money by planting sparsely and allowing room for the plants to develop gradually to their full size. Get a catalogue from a nursery specializing in flowering shrubs and find the heights of the various specimens. This will give you the cue to the room each shrub needs. A shrub that grows to a height of 6 ft usually needs 3 ft on either side, for instance, in which to spread, and one which grows to 4 ft needs about 2 ft.

The number of shrubs and the height used largely depends on the size of the garden and the width of the border. For the smaller garden, buy the dwarf types, while for the larger garden it is possible to have borders 12 ft wide. Arrange the taller shrubs at the back, the medium-growing types in the middle and the smaller ones towards the front. Put the earlier-flowering evergreens mainly towards the back where later in the year, they will be hidden by the deciduous late-flowering shrubs growing nearer the front.

In many ways there is no cheaper form of gardening – in the long run. The actual cost of the shrubs may be high, but over twenty-five years the cost is indeed low. The border is permanent and can be very beautiful. Lilies and bulbs like snowdrops, daffodils and crocuses can be planted amongst the shrubs if desired, while the blue Tibetan poppies can be used to give depth of colour in between the shrub groups. Shrubs form an excellent screen to hide the next-door neighbours' washing, or that ugly fence. This flowering screen protects against the cold winds and can also provide attractive scents, not forgetting the berries and catkins on individual shrubs in the autumn and winter.

The shrub border needs no special preparation but of course must be initially free from perennial weeds. These can be eliminated by using one of the strong weed killers before planting. Apply organic matter such as compost or sedge peat all over the ground after planting, to conserve moisture and feed the soil organisms below, as well as smother all the annual weeds.

A very light forking may be necessary and if the soil is heavy a subsequent rake-over to get the bed level. It is in such a prepared bed that the flowering shrubs are planted.

Those who cannot afford to buy all the shrubs needed in the first year should plant *the slower growing kinds the first season*, the next slowest growers the following year and the quick growing types like the shrub roses and brooms the third year. If the border is wide it pays to plant in groups of three or four of a kind. Never plant single specimens in a repetitive fashion all down a border, making it look regimented.

With the small shrubs, form drifts of four or five of a species and in very large borders of five or six. With medium-sized shrubs three will make a nice group, but in the case of narrow borders, and with the broad spreading specimens, one should do.

As these groups of shrubs 'drift' naturally and happily towards one another, remember that there should be some background for the deciduous shrubs. Such a border may otherwise look depressing in the winter because there is no series of evergreen shrubs acting as a background to the border. Flowering evergreens are ideal for this purpose, for even after the blooms have fallen and the birds have eaten the berries of fruits, the leaves remain.

A gardener should be an artist craftsman. He must think of his colours, heights and shapes and group them attractively. He must balance the foreground against the background. He should know that a mass of small flowers looks more wonderful at a distance than one or two large ones. It is important to satisfy the eye.

In some gardens there may be some objects at a distance or even in the plot next door that must be screened off and for this the taller shrubs and tree may be used.

There are a number of flowering trees like *Prunus serrulata erecta* which grow like church spires and never spread. They are covered with blossoms in the spring so the gardener can have masses of flowers 'in the air' without robbing the shrubs below of light.

Some shrubs never mind being planted close together. At Arkley Manor, *The Good Gardeners' Association* is purposely demonstrating three or four of these types. These are:

1 *Kurumé Azaleas*, so wonderful in a mass,
2 Dwarf Rhododendrons, greatly admired by visitors
3 *Ericas*, referred to in Chapter 11
4 *Cotoneasters*, (in particular *Cotoneaster horizontalis*),

which scramble over the surface of the ground and are delightful when fully berried in the autumn and winter. The many members of the *Berberis* family can also be massed if necessary.

Despite the close planting of these five types it may be necessary to thin out because one shrub gets in the way of another. After five or six years harden your heart and with a pair of secateurs cut the branches back cleanly, just at a joint where a suitable lateral or side growth is developing.

Details of individual varieties of shrub can be found in the list at the end of this chapter. Remember, however, there are species and varieties which dislike lime or do not care for soils which are not acid. If you have chalky or limestone land, keep away from rhododendrons, azaleas, kalmias, andromedas, pieris and many of the heathers.

Planting Shrubs must be planted firmly. After spreading the roots out, covering with soil treading down firmly and staking it if necessary, spread the area with sedge peat an inch deep. Tread this down well and no hoeing should be necessary. The peat will smother the weeds, and provide the perfect mulch, supplying organic matter needed by the denizens of the soil.

The alternative to brown powdery compost or sedge peat is fresh leaves. These should be swept up the moment they have fallen and put all over the shrub border to the depth of 4 in. The leaves must be beaten down well with a fork or the back of a spade, and if the weather is dry, must be well watered.

Those who employ tidy-minded, old fashioned gardeners who invariably want to rake up the leaves and burn them must watch out. Never allow this. Fresh leaves are the most useful alternative to sedge peat. The leaves are apt to blow about however, and the answer lies in laying them deeply enough and thickly enough. 4 in is right: if they are only an inch deep they may blow away.

With dwarf shrubs like *Kurumé azaleas* and baby rhododendrons a thick mat of leaves is not possible and medium grade sedge peat should be used. The powdered bark of forest trees is used an inch deep all over the area occupied by the azaleas. Such a dressing encourages the roots of the plants to come right to the surface of the ground and because of the top dressing these roots need never be disturbed by a fork or hoe.

Remember flowering shrubs largely look after themselves and a border such as this will save much toil.

List of hardy, easy to grow shrubs

Name	Description	Time of flowering
Andromeda floribunda	Lily-of-the-Valley shrub	March–April
Arbutus unedo	Evergreen bearing strawberry-like fruits	May–June
Azaleas	Evergreen in variety	
Berberis aquifolium	Grows well in either full sun or in shade; beautiful colour in the autumn; evergreen	April–May
Berberis bealei	The large-flowered form, long leaves, evergreen	March–April
Berberis darwinii	Rich orange flowers and glossy leaves, purple berries, evergreen	May
Berberis stenophylla	Long drooping branches covered with yellow flowers, evergreen	May
Berberis thunbergii	A lovely plant in the spring; blossoms pale straw colour	May
Berberis thunbergii atropurpurea	A rich foliage, bronze-red colour	May
Berberis thunbergii erecta	A new form with upright growth	May
Berberis wilsonae	Dwarf habit highly coloured in autumn	May
Buddleia alternifolia	Arching branches, covered with small fragrant mauve flowers	June–July
Buddleia globosa	Evergreen, tall attractive shrub with orange ball-like flowers	May

Name	Description	Flowering time
Buddleia magnifica	A fine form with long purple spikes	July–September
Ceanothus burkwoodii	Choice late-flowering variety, masses of rich blue flowers	July–October
Ceanothus dentatus	Bright blue flowers in the spring	February–June
Choisya ternata (Mexican Orange)	Evergreen, white scented flowers	May
Cytisus andreanus	Yellow and crimson	May
Cytisus burkwoodii	Cerise and maroon	May
Cytisus fulgens	Amber and red	May
Colutea arborescens (Bladder Senna)	Yellow flowers	July–September
Cotoneaster franchetii	Evergreen, silver reverse plus orange-coloured berries	September–October
Daphne mezereum	An early-flowering species. Clusters of red flowers	February
Deutzia candidissima	Double, white flowers	June–July
Deutzia rosea	Soft carmine–rose	June –July
Erica carnea C. J. Backhouse	Pale pink, 6 in	April
Erica ciliaris globosa	Rose-pink, 6 in	August–October
Erica vagans Lyonesse	White, 18 in	August–September
Escallonia langleyensis	Pink flowers; evergreen, shiny leaves	June–July
Escallonia macrantha	A rich carmine; evergreen, broad leaves	June–July

59

Name	Description	Time of Flowering
Forsythia intermedia	A fairly upright grower; rich yellow blooms	March–April
Fuchsia riccartonii	Crimson and purple flowers	July–October
Hamamelis mollis (Witch Hazel)	Yellow flowers in large clusters	December
Hibiscus rubis	Single, rich crimson	August–November
Hibiscus syriacus	Various colours	August–November
Hydrangea hortensis	All varieties, pot grown	from July
Hydrangea paniculata grandiflora	Creamy white flowers turning pink; hardy	August–September
Kalmia latifolia (Mountain Laurel)	Evergreen; attractive pink flower	June
Kerria japonica flore pleno (Batchelor's Buttons)	Large, double, yellow flowers	April–May
Laburnum (Golden Chain)	Very long racemes of flowers	May–June
Laburnum vossii	Beautiful white glistening flowers	May–June
Magnolia grandiflora	Evergreen; masses of white flowers in late summer	August–September
Olearia haastii (Daisy Bush)	Single dwarf erect growth; fragrant	June–July
Philadelphus lemoinei erectus	One of the best scented	June–July
Philadelphus 'Virginal'	A dwarf-growing shrub yellow flowers	May–September
Potentilla ferreri	White flowers	May –September
Potentilla veitchii		
Rhus cotinus Royal Purple (Smoke Tree)	Smoky-copper foliage	Spring, summer, Autumn

Ribes atrosanguineum	This form has deep blood-red flowers	April
Rosmarinus officinalis	Grey leaves, blue flowers, evergreen	May–June
Senecio greyii	Evergreen; silver-grey foliage; yellow flowers	July–August
Skimmia japonica	Evergreen; small white flowers in spring; red berries in winter	April–May
Spiraea douglasii	Red flowers 4–8 in	July–August
Spiraea thunbergii	Early-flowering variety; white	March–April
Taxmarix pentandra	Bright pink	July
Veronica salicifolia	White spikes; evergreen	June–July
Veronica traversii	Hardy; white flowers; evergreen	July
Viburnum burkwoodii	Fragrant white flowers; evergreen	April–May
Viburnum carlesii	Sweetly-scented white flowers	April–May
Viburnum opulus (Guelder Rose)	Red berries	May–June
Weigela florida variegata	Pink flowers	May–June
Weigela rosea	Bright rose-pink	May–June

8 Hedges

The idea here is to make a hedge of good thick shrubs to form an effective but easily managed barrier between one garden and another, or perhaps between the garden and a field below. An ordinary hedge has to be cut twice a year and though the Tarpen Hedge Trimmer described in Chapter 17 saves three-quarters of the work, there is still some labour needed. The alternative to the hedge of course is to erect an overlap larch fence, because this provides 6 ft of immediate privacy.

Those who desire a beautiful live hedge however, must choose, where possible, shrubs that flower on the side shoots and moreover grow fairly slowly. The varieties chosen must not need constant trimming, only an occasional pruning back with secateurs.

The informal hedge is not planted like the ordinary hedge in straight lines. Though it may look ragged to start with, the shrubs will form a privacy hedge eventually, and the idea is to get a hedge that looks 'natural'. The author has had wonderful hedges formed with Penzance Briars which are covered with pink and red roses in the summer and scented leaves in the winter. In the south and south-west of England, especially near the sea, fuchsia hedges are often used and look beautiful. Hedges can be colourful as well as fulfilling their function of keeping out unwanted visitors, offering protection from the winds and keeping the garden secluded.

It is wise to discuss this type of hedge with a local nurseryman. Some shrubs do well in the south-west but fail in the north. No arbitrary division can be made of north versus south but obtain good local advice from a nursery.

By getting the right shrubs and by buying the necessary varieties it should be possible to have an informal hedge

with many flowers blooming from the beginning of
February to the middle of November.

Actual planting As with the shrub border, it is only
necessary to fork over lightly the strip of ground required
and to add at the same time powdery compost or
medium-grade sedge peat at two or three bucketfuls
to the square yard. The shrubs will not be planted in
straight lines so the strip of land prepared may have to be
3 or 4 ft wide. The disadvantage of the informal hedge is
that it takes up more lateral room than a formal one. The
alternative method is to plant the hedge in a cleared strip
of soil and then to mulch the ground on either side of
the hedge with powdery compost an inch deep.

Plant closer on the whole than in the shrub border as the
idea is to get the shrubs to overlap and ensure privacy.
Where one would normally plant 4 ft apart in the flowering shrub border, in the informal hedge the planting
would be at 3 ft apart. Plant in October, or at latest early
November, so that the roots will establish while the soil
is warm and send out new root hairs before the winter.

Spread the roots out well but not deeply. Look for the
soil mark on the stems and plant to a similar depth.
Tread well, wearing heavy boots, and then rake lightly so
as to level. Apply a top dressing of home-made compost
or sedge peat an inch deep all over the strip of ground.
This will save labour and produce the natural conditions
the shrubs love.

If it is desired to have a quick screen then larger and
taller shrubs may be planted. These may need staking for
the first year or two. Use chestnut stakes which have been
dipped in green Rentokil fluid for five or six hours, drive
them in near the shrub stem and attach the one to the other
by means of a Rainbow plastic strap tie. These Rainbow
ties are ideal because they are quick to apply and give
as the shrub stem grows.

It is wise to plant the spring-flowering shrubs alternately with the summer-flowering kinds. This mixture

ensures there is some colour right down the hedge for most of the year. The author has been experimenting with shrubs as informal hedges for fifteen years and the following list includes both the evergreen and deciduous shrubs that have done well in minimum-work gardens up and down the country.

Informal Hedge Shrubs

Name	Description	Height
Acer palmatum atropurpureum	Strong growing, low-spreading, bearing bronze–crimson leaves throughout summer.	4–5 ft
Acer palmatum flavescens	Similar to above, bears variegated cream yellow leaves; not suitable for the colder parts.	4–5 ft
Acer palmatum Osakazuki	Typical Japanese maple; fiery scarlet foliage in autumn.	4–5 ft
Arbutus unedo	Strawberry tree, tasteless fruits, similar in shape and colour to a strawberry; good shrub for coastal districts.	8–10 ft
Berberis thunbergii atropurpurea	Free flowering; produces reddish purple autumn foliage and scarlet berries; compact.	5 ft
Camellia japonica chandleri elegans	Hardy as laurel; large light rose flowers with paeony centre.	4–5 ft
Camellia japonica Jupiter	Bears large single flowers; 'geranium' coloured; vigorous grower.	4–5 ft
Cotoneaster franchetii	Hardy, ornamental shrub; greyish foliage; orange–scarlet berries.	2–3 ft
Cotoneaster frigida	Similar to above clusters of crimson berries in autumn and winter.	4–5 ft
Cotoneaster microphyllus	Small glossy-leaved evergreen; extra large red berries; prostrate in growth.	5–6 ft
Grevillea rosmarinifolia	Bears crimson flowers in summer on long racemes; suitable for mild areas.	6 ft

Name	Description	Height
Myrtus communis	This is the common myrtle; bears masses of white flowers in July; hardy.	12 ft
Myrtus obcordata	Good hardy myrtle; green downy leaves, flowers in summer followed by a violet berry.	10–15 ft
Olearia gunniana splendens	Tasmanian daisy bush; flowers in May; like a Michaelmas Daisy in appearance; there are blue, rose and lavender varieties	
Pernettya mucronata Bell's Seedling	Showy dwarfish evergreen, produces a thicket; flowers heath-like, extra large and white, followed by dark red marble-like berries, must be grown in non-limy soil.	5 ft
Pernettya mucronata Davis' Hybrids	Similar to above, but bears large berries in many colours.	5–6 ft
Phillyrea vilmoriniana	Evergreen shrub; produces dome-shaped bush with globular leaves; bears fragrant white flowers in clusters in the spring, followed by purplish black fruits.	5–6 ft
Pyracantha angustifolia	One of the firethorns; bears hawthorn-like flowers in early summer and clusters of orange berries in the autumn; leaves narrow, grey felt beneath.	8–10 ft
Pyracantha coccinea lalandii	Bears large orange-red berries in autumn and winter.	6-8 ft
Rhododendrons: Gomer Waterer	White, slightly blushed flowers; flowers in May.	
Rhododendrons: John Walter	Rosy-crimson flowers; flowers early June.	
Rhododendrons: Britannia	Bright crimson-red, flowers slow growing, rounded habit; May–early June.	

Rhododendrons: Mrs. de Bruin	Carmine-red; flowers early June.	
Rhododendrons: Mrs R. S. Holford	Rosy salmon; flowers May–early June.	
Rose Species: *hugonis	Single yellow	
Rose Species: moyesii	Scarlet } followed by attractive hips.	4–5 ft
Rose Species: nevada	Creamy white, large	
Skimmia japonica	Compact slow-growing shrub which prefers shade; bears scarlet berries on female plants; grand for town gardens; advisable to plant male and female plants	4–5 ft
Veronica brachysiphon	Flowers in July, white; invaluable for seaside and the south and west.	
Veronica carnea	Bears rosy-pink flowers from May to late summer	4 ft
Veronica Hieland Lassie	Very hardy; bears violet-blue flowers from July to September.	3–4 ft
Veronica hulkeana	Pale lavender-blue flowers, 1 ft long; only grows in south-west.	3–4 ft
Veronica lindsayi	Very hardy; dense-growing, pink-flowered.	3–4 ft

*Other rose species are described in my book, *The Basic Book of Roses* published by Barrie & Jenkins.

9 A Henry VIII wild garden

A wild garden can easily be the mini-work gardener's dream. It hasn't got to look posh and spruced up. The plants that are grown can be allowed to develop as they will. There need be no pruning, no spraying, no hoeing, forking or digging, and yet the garden can look attractive and can certainly be very restful. The idea is to accept the garden as it is. It may be that builders have left a grass pasture and if so, use it as it is. If, on the other hand, the soil is cultivated, then just get it as level as possible and sow some grass seed literally everywhere.

The Henry VIII wild garden merely consists of wandering grass paths, which are kept cut low with a Flymo or rotary mower. These wander about in between flowering shrubs which themselves are growing in grass. The paths however are always kept mown low as a lawn, but the sward where the shrubs are growing is kept cut to a height of about 3 in.

At convenient spots natural elm seats are provided so that people may sit in seclusion and admire nature's handiwork. A wild garden can be very peaceful, and is a wonderful place in the summer to get away from the hurly-burly of a busy business world. In the attractive and soothing wild garden, there can be a tiny little copse planted, say, with silver birch, and growing among the trees there may be bluebells, primroses, cowslips, ferns, plus many specimens of plants which we normally call wild flowers.

The basis then of the wild garden is grass. The trees and shrubs grow, so to speak, in a roughly cut pasture. When first planted a little circle of soil is left around them to ensure that the specimens do not starve in the early stages. Later, the mowings from the grass paths can be used as a mulch over the little circle of soil.

Of course, it is easier when a new house is built in a

woodland area. It is a pity to grub up the trees in order to make a formal garden. The little clumps of trees that are already there can be used with great effect. A wild garden must look natural – and appear to have a 'just grown' look. It should be planted so that it needs the minimum of management, and if the whole of the garden cannot be devoted to wildness, consider making just a part of it into a Henry VIII garden, if you can find a site that is secluded.

Those who wish to develop such a garden in a treeless area must be guided by the setting and plant the trees and shrubs that suit it best. It is wise to try and discover the trees and shrubs that are indigenous to the district. It may be rhododendron land, so to speak, or it may be that the soil is first class for willows. It could be cherry country, with opportunities for trees with coloured barks as well as wonderful flowers. One can often learn much by chatting to a local head gardener of a big house nearby, or to the oldest inhabitant, or a park superintendent. Looking at gardens nearby is often educative, and the gardening correspondent of the local paper may be able to give excellent advice.

Of course there will be no hoeing and no weeding in this grassland wild garden. Small hand scythes or sickles will keep down any grass that is too tufty and tall or if the area is a large one, one of the rotary cutters used four or five times a year over the rough grass will keep it in pasture condition.

The layout is largely a matter of taste but it is good to give the idea of length by having a winding path. This might traverse from one end of the garden to the other, allowing a vista to be seen, however narrow. Once the main trees and shrubs have been put in, the area can be under-planted so as to have something of interest to show all the year round. Visits to the countryside will give ideas. For instance, although it is useful to have evergreens like *Laurustinus* to give seclusion when other trees are bare, it is also wise to have shrubs that bear berries and fruits in the autumn. This makes for beauty and interest.

When a wild garden has to be made from scratch, medium-grade sedge peat may be used around the base of the trees and shrubs in a circle, after planting firmly. After this, the fallen leaves and grass mowings will provide some protection for the roots, as well as most of the humus they need.

The wild garden will never be a garish, ultra-colourful garden. It is, so to speak, a woodland garden and the aim is to use plants that prefer the semi-shade and love the high organic content of the leaf mould.

Lime soils When the soil is very limy it is impossible to grow rhododendrons, azaleas or heathers.

Some people try to alter limy soil and force the 'lime haters' to grow. They do this either by forking in flowers of sulphur at a $\frac{1}{4}$ lb to the square yard or aluminium sulphate at $\frac{1}{2}$ lb to the square yard. I much prefer to stick to trees, shrubs and plants which are happy in this particular soil rather than introduce 'foreigners' and attempt to make the soil suitable for them.

Those who have never made a wild garden should go to the country so that they can walk through a copse or woodland glade to see what it is like. With this picture in mind the keen gardener can return home and try to produce what he has seen on a smaller scale. Don't plant the trees too close, and on the score of expense, start with small specimens which will grow large later on and remember that they will need plenty of room.

Naturalizing bulbs Wild gardens are first class for naturalizing bulbs; that is, planting them and letting them go on growing for years without disturbing them. You can have large drifts of daffodils, and some nurserymen offer bulbs by the hundredweight comparatively cheaply for naturalizing purposes. The plan is to take the bulbs out of the bag in which they come and throw them gently onto the grass to grow exactly where they fall. Thus one ensures they look as natural as possible when they flower. It is a great mistake to plant in squares, rounds or triangles. Similarly, it is possible to plant bluebells, crocuses, snowdrops and those lovely golden yellow winter aconites which flower beautifully in January and are not too expensive or difficult.

It is impossible to think of a wild garden without great drifts of primroses and cowslips. Raise the plants from seed and place them in natural groups where they are to grow; otherwise buy them as plants to ensure quicker results. Remember that once they are established they will seed and so increase. There are also pink and white foxgloves, which are happy in shade. Some have flowers that are attractively spotted.

The wood anemone is among the most exquisite of our woodland flowers as is the dog-toothed violet, both the white and the blue. Plant also the dainty little harebell that masses in a light, stony soil, and evening primroses (or *Oenotheras*) remembering that they like a little spot where the sun trickles through the leaves of the trees above. Valerian flowers well in a chalky soil and Whin or Grose can be planted on sandy land where there is chalk underneath. Baby cyclamen may be allowed to nestle around some of the trees and the Christmas rose will thrive in some of the shady spots.

Wild flower seeds There are some seeds of wild flowers available and readers who have difficulty in getting supplies may write to the author. Only a small percentage of these seeds may grow but once established they will self-seed. For instance, it is possible to sow seeds of the Common Yarrow. There is also a very strong-growing species of a wild mignonette (*Reseda alba*) bearing long spikes of whitish flowers. The woodland tulip (*Tulip silvestris*) is fascinating. The perianth is bright yellow and about 2 in long and the flowers are very fragrant.

Another way to get hold of wild flowers is to go to the country and pick from the hedgerows the seed-pods of any you see. These can be sown immediately where the flowers are to be grown, or they can be sown in boxes in the greenhouse and put out in natural drifts later. When sowing out of doors, do so very shallowly. Remember, in the normal way the seeds drop on the surface of the ground.

Wild grasses One can also concentrate on the ornamental grasses and these can be most attractive. There is Love Grass for instance, Squirrel-tailed Grass, Cloud Grass, Quaking Grass, Feather Grass and so on. The seeds of these grasses can be bought for about 20p a packet and are very useful for floral art in the home.

This is indeed minimum work It will be seen that there is little work to do in the wild garden other than to keep the 2 ft wide wandering path cut say once a week. Such a path should never be straight or otherwise it will not be possible to provide secluded corners for the seats provided. The flowering shrubs should never be planted in straight lines, but should go in so that they grow in their individual positions, looking natural. Plan ahead so that the grass path may have to curve round a shrub, giving the appearance that the meander was made necessary by the shrub. Actually, of course, the gardener planted the shrub there to make the reason for the curve.

Fortunately, there are no hard and fast rules as to how a wild garden must be planned or planted, this must be left to the individual taste of the garden owner. Do go and see a wild garden that has been established at Arkley Manor and this will give you one idea of what can be done.

In the spring of course, the wild garden will be alight with drifts of bluebells, golden splashes of daffodils, pretty primroses, baby jonquils, and any other suitable bulbs that the owner may like to 'naturalize'. There are bulb firms, in fact, which specialize in providing inexpensive selections of bulbs for naturalizing purposes in wild gardens.

10 Roses

No plant has gripped the imagination of amateur gardeners more than the rose. There has been an even greater interest since the introduction of the Floribunda types which flower from June to October. It can be said, too, that the dwarf types of the Floribundas are popular as permanent bedding plants which saves the constant planning out in spring and autumn, for these roses stay put.

In any minimum-work garden there is no need to do any deep-digging but remember that if the soil is water-logged the roses won't grow. When the soil lies sodden in winter the lower roots are killed. The minimum-work gardener must avoid roses if he has soil like this, unless he has the garden drained properly by an outside contractor.

For ten years the author experimented at Thaxted and found that roses need no digging, so long as ample quantities of organic matter were applied to a depth of at least an inch all over the ground. In fact, at Arkley Manor there has been no digging at all in seventeen years. A hole sufficiently wide and deep is made to accommodate the roots of the rose bush and that is all. The worms then do any deep digging that may be necessary. They pull some of the fine organic matter (that has been put on as a mulch) into the soil lower down, and this is converted by the soil bacteria into humus.

Those who insist on digging should do it (in the case of heavy land) before the end of October. This allows the soil to settle before the roots have to go in. With light land anyone can plant up to the end of November. Some people even plant as late as early March, but the author never advises this because the bushes do not get a good start.

Any soil that is prepared for roses must first be cleared of perennial weeds: S.B.K. or similar liquid hormone, used in accordance with the maker's instructions, will clear any land of most of these. In bad cases, however, it is advisable to carry out this weed treatment during a period of six months and then to allow another six months to elapse before the planting.

When raking the soil level, apply a fish or seaweed fertilizer at 3 or 4 ozs to the square yard. Organic fertilizers may be applied as well, at 1 oz to the square yard, once a fortnight from 1st May to 15th June. In sandy soil it is a good thing to add wood ashes at 8 ozs to the square yard. Do not attempt to plant roses during frosty weather and do not prune them until after planting – except those put in the ground in March. All roses must be pruned carefully to just above a bud. If they are cut back hard the first year, it does help to establish the rose trees quickly.

In order to spread the roots out carefully and properly, make a hole about 15 in square and 6 in deep. This also enables you to see that the point at which the budding was done is just below the surface of the ground, when the bed has been firmed down well. Don't ever allow the roots to be doubled up against the side of the hole. If they are too long, cut them back carefully with a sharp pair of secateurs. Never plant when it is really wet because it is impossible to get the sodden soil firm afterwards.

It is best to plant the strong varieties of bush roses 20 in apart and the dwarf kinds 18 in apart so a mass of blooms is produced and the soil below is hardly seen at all. The stronger Floribundas need to be planted 2 ft square. Dwarf Floribundas can go in 18 in square.

Once the planting has been done *firmly* (this is vital), the surface of the soil must be covered with an inch of sedge peat. Sedge peat can be used entirely for this purpose, but a more economical way is to put on a half-inch depth of good vegetable compost peat first, and top it up with the sedge peat afterwards.

If the coarse sedge peat is used the birds tend to take it to make their nests and this naturally makes the rose garden untidy. Use medium-grade sedge peat and the

PLATE 7. The rose beds at Arkley Manor are mulched with powdery compost 1 inch deep, and so annual weeds are avoided.

birds don't see it. In fact, the medium-grade can normally be used all the time and every time as a top dressing so that the annual weeds are smothered and the earth cannot fully dry out, even in a drought.

The sedge peat also helps to create a barrier for the spores of the black spot that may be in the soil, which in the ordinary way blow up from the earth onto the leaves in the spring; mulch usually prevents both this disease and mildew.

The sedge peat must completely cover the bed and not just be put around the bushes. Some people use lawn mowings instead but these are not weed-free and so can cause trouble, and, if fresh mowings are put on too thickly they can heat up as they decompose and damage the roses. Sedge peat like good compost is weed-free, pest-free and disease-free, and as it is rich in humus the roses revel in it.

The original quantity of the compost raked into the soil before planting will not keep the roses going for the next ten years. The minimum-work gardener therefore provides plant food in organic form in the simplest way. He sprinkles the fish or seaweed fertilizer at the rate of 3 to 4 ozs to the square yard all over the sedge peat each February, and where the growth of the roses does not appear as good as it ought to be, more of these organic fertilizers may be given at 1 oz to the square yard as has been said earlier on. These fertilizers are gradually washed in through the peat to give the roses a steady source of extra food.

Once the beds or roses are properly planted and properly mulched there is little or no work to be done for the next ten years. Each season, pruning will be necessary: some people believe in delaying this until April, others do it boldly in December. In the instance of the H.T. roses, it is usual to cut back the growths after the first general blooming in June, which means reducing the length of the flowering branches by about 8 ins. The second blooming should therefore take place in September. It is never advisable to cut back further than this, or the bases of the buds will be encouraged to grow and these may be killed by the frosts in the winter months.

If pests and diseases occur, the simplest way of spraying with the insecticides or fungicides is to use a Solo or knapsack sprayer. The right amount of liquid Derris for different pests will be indicated on the label. The bushes are then given a thorough soaking, but everything should be done to encourage the predators like ladybirds.

Varieties There are a very large number of varieties to choose from and the author has purposely chosen kinds which require the minimum of attention. For further details as regards varieties, the reader might like to consult his book, *The Basic Book of Rose Growing*.

Name	*Description*
	Hybrid Teas
Alec's Red	A perfectly shaped, many petalled rose. Fully scented.
Amazing Grace	Forty-five petals in each delicately scented bloom. Flowers plentifully.
Apricot Silk	Well formed blooms of sheened apricot. Ideal for cutting.
Bettina	Orange with a flush of red and veined with bronze.
Blue Moon	Huge ice-blue blooms with an unusual lemon perfume.
Bon-Accord	Compact medium growing bush. Very fragrant.
Chicago Peace	'Peace' but blooms richer in colour – soft pink with reverse petal copper yellow.
Duke of Windsor	Medium sized blooms of delicate luminous orange.
Drambuie	A beautiful, fragrant, deep amber bloom.
Fragrant Cloud	Deep coral red with a foil of dark green foliage. Disease-resistant.
George Dickson	Very fragrant: rich crimson vigorous up-right growth.
Gold Crown	Deep golden yellow with reddish flush. Disease-resistant.
Grandpa Dickson	Lemon yellow blooms. Disease-resistant foliage.
Grandmere Jenny	A new race of rose combining delightful form and colour with lovely fresh fragrance.
Invitation	Large heavily scented blooms on long stems. Clear rose with outside petal a lighter rose shade suffused with gold.
Josephine Bruce	Medium sized blooms of dark, velvety crimson – very free flowering.
King's Ransom	Superb foliage and beautiful yellow blooms.
Ladies Choice	A fragrant, strong growing beauty with elegant buds opening to perfect blooms.
Mischief	Perfectly shaped buds opening to coral-salmon blooms.
Miss Harp	Unfading, deep golden-yellow, classically perfect from bud to open flower. Long stemmed.

Name	*Description*
Mrs. Sam McGredy	Large coppery-orange blooms; attractive bronzy foliage.
My Love	A fine, dark red rose. Superbly fragrant.
Papa Meilland	Large blooms of a rich, deep velvety crimson. Old rose fragrance.
Peace	Large yellow blooms with a flush of pink on petal edges. Never prune this variety hard.
Piccadilly	Bright scarlet on the inside and gold on outside when in bud: the scarlet suffuses through the gold as they open.
Rose Gaujard	An enormous rose-red with copper veining.
Royal Highness	Soft light pink blooms; disease-resistant foliage; fragrant.
Sam McGredy	Honey-yellow changes to dark cream; base sunflower yellow.
Summer Sunshine	Dazzling yellow which remains clear and brilliant to the last petal.
Super Star	Overflowing with delightful sweet fragrance. Free flowering with shiny green foliage.
Wendy Cussons	A very pleasing cerise, really fragrant.
Whisky Mac	Deep harvest-gold, bronzed in the bud.

Floribundas

All Gold	Deep gold-yellow remains from opening of the bud to petal drop.
Anna Wheatcroft	Pale vermilion with gold stamens. Disease-resistant.
Chanelle	Semi-double scented blooms of cream; shaded yellow base.
Daily Sketch	Plum-red and silver. Strong, healthy plant of medium size.
Dearest	Clear, soft rosy-salmon of perfect form.
Elizabeth of Glamis	Salmon-pink in colour and sweetly scented.
Golden Slippers	A golden floribunda of great merit. Dainty, miniature, perfectly formed, hybrid, tea-type blooms.
Heaven Scent	Glowing crimson scarlet. Very full blooms with a wonderful fragrance.

Name	Description
Honeymoon	Pure yellow of lasting colour. Large, very healthy light green foliage.
Ivory Fashion	Pale cream to deep yellow; semi-double blooms.
John Church	Fragrant blooms of orange-salmon. Disease-resistant.
Korona	A vivid vermilion scarlet that does not fade. Foliage almost evergreen.
Lavender Lassie	Sweetly scented rose bearing a profusion of huge trusses (flower clusters) in lavender pink.
Meggiddo	Luminous orange-red flowers, shiny green foliage. A radiant beauty.
Moulin Rouge	Non-fading scarlet blooms. Late flowering.
Nan Anderson	Clean clear pink with a coral sheen.
Orange Sensation	A glowing orange-vermilion rose produced on large trusses.
Paddy McGredy	Deep coral pink, vigorous healthy plant scented.
Sea Pearl	Pearl pink blooms: outer side of petal is suffused with peach and sulphur yellow shadings.

ROSE SPECIES AS BORDER SHRUBS

The great advantage of Species Rose borders is that no pruning in the strict sense of the word is necessary, and for months the border needs little attention. It may be necessary each spring to go round with secateurs to cut out some dead wood, or to prune back some of the tips that have been damaged by the frost, but that is easy. There may be a few rose shrubs that need to be kept within bounds because they are taking up too much space but it does not take a moment to reduce their branches a little. Others may be getting out of shape, and a cut here and there will put this right.

It is best to plant the rose shrubs on the lines advised for the planting of the border in Chapter 7: that is, do not plant only one kind of shrub, but have about three in a group unless the border is small. Naturally the gardener will plant the dwarf varieties at the front and the taller kinds at the back; and if the border is central, with grass on either side, the shorter species will be planted on the outside and the taller ones towards the middle. The advantage of this is that all the plants get plenty of light and air. I recommend the planting of 'double-faced' borders wherever possible.

Plant the dwarf types in drifts, putting the taller ones in the centre because they take up so much room. Aim for a splash of colour, and arrange the planting so that no long length of bed is lacking in interest for long. This is comparatively easy with roses, because most of them flower for many months, and many produce fascinating fruits which are a delight in the autumn and winter.

The following are some of the rose species that might be included. They are my favourites, and I can recommend them.

Species Roses

Name	*Description*
Common Provence	Rose-pink; fragrant.
Crimson Damask	Crimson; sweetly-scented.
Frühlingsgold	Cream with golden centre; wild rose scent; single.
Maiden's Blush	Flesh pink flowers with darker centre; fragrant.
Rosa anthina (Canary Bird)	Compact – 4 to 5 ft. Large, clear yellow flowers.
Rosa bella	Attractive. 6 ft. Cherry red flowers; fragrant.
Rosa blanda	Thornless. 6 ft. Pink flowers 2 in across.
Rosa chinensis mutablis	Small, upright, single flowers, 3 to 4 in across: buff-shaded carmine, changing to rose and finally crimson.

Name	Description
Rosa dupontii	9 ft. Large flowers 3 in wide: blush to creamy white; fragrant.
Rosa farreri	Spreading. 6 ft. Small pink or white flowers; bright coral-red fruits; dainty fern-like foliage.
Rosa fendleri	5 ft. Densely leaved; large lilac-pink flowers; large sealing-wax red hips.
Rosa foliolosa	Less than 3 ft. Pink fragrant flowers, $1\frac{1}{2}$ to 2 in across; red orange-shaped fruits, late flowering.
Rosa hibernica	Delicate shell-pink flowers, 2 in across, carried June, single or in pairs.
Rosa hugonis	Graceful. 6 ft. Soft yellow flowers on long arching branches; delicate fern-like foliage.
Rosa moyesii	8–10 ft. Rich blood-crimson flowers $2\frac{1}{2}$ to 3 in across; large crimson flagon-shaped fruits in autumn.
Rosa mundi	Flowers red striped with white.
Rosa nevada	6–7 ft. Single flowers 4 in across: pale pink opening to creamy white.
Rosa pisocarpa	Slender, lilac-pink flowers $1\frac{1}{4}$ in across in clusters; sea-green foliage.
Rosa pratii	6 ft. Dainty foliage. Rose flowers: clusters of crimson; bottle-shaped fruits.
Rosa primula	Primrose-yellow flowers passing to white in mid-May. Incense-like odour.
Rosa rubrifolia	Pink blooms. Valuable for its decorative foliage.
Rosa sancta	Low growing, shell-pink, slightly fragrant, flowers up to 3 in across in loose clusters.
Rosa spinossisima	3–4 ft. Small white flowers; black fruits.
Rosa stellata mirifica	Rare, small, solitary rose-purple flowers; red fruits; branches crowded with ivory-coloured prickles.
Rosa virginiana	5 ft. Large pink flowers; glossy foliage turning brilliant crimson.
Rosa wichuraiana	Sub-evergreen. Small leaves, small white flowers.
York and Lancaster	White, striped red.

11 No work with a heather garden

There is perhaps no easier type of garden to manage than one planted with heathers. Once the plants are put in and the ground is covered with powdery compost or sedge peat there is little or no work to do. It is true that keen gardeners cut off the flowers immediately blossoming is over, but even that can be done quickly with a pair of shears. There are types and varieties of heathers which will flower almost every month of the year and a heather bank or bed can therefore be attractive week after week throughout the year.

SOILS

Many people imagine that heathers can only be grown on acid soils rich in peat, but this is not true. There are varieties of heather which will put up with a limy soil and others will grow in a soil that is not acid, providing a good quantity of sedge peat is forked in first. The idea is to plant the heathers and allow them to spread: then they smother the weeds, yet look very attractive.

Of course, there are chalky or limestony soils where the growing of heathers is not easy. I know gardens above the cliffs of Dover, for instance, where there is only a few inches of soil with yards and yards of chalk below. In such shallow soils over chalk, a tremendous amount of peat would be needed to get any good results at all – plus applications of, say, *Sequestrene*. However, in normal limy soils, the plan is to grow the winter-flowering *Erica carnea*, the larger summer flowering *Erica terminalis* and *Erica mediterranea*, as well as the hybrid known as *Erica darleyensis*.

Those who say it is impossible to grow heathers in

heavy clay soils should know that at Thaxted, Essex, where the soil is of this type, 'rivers of heathers' were grown in such a soil, once it had been enriched with sedge peat, at three large bucketfuls to the square yard. The term 'rivers' is used because the heathers were planted in continuous groups, so as to look like streams flowing from the top of the bank to the grass below.

With these few reservations, heathers can be grown on almost any soil and the only thing the plants need in plenty is sun. Heathers are rarely attacked by pests or diseases, so there is no spraying or dusting to do. However, rabbits will go for the younger plants when they are *first* put out, so if you live in a rabbit infested area – beware.

PLANTING TIME

The best time for planting is in late September or early October, but it is possible to plant any time in the winter. By planting before the soil is cold the roots get a hold and it is not long before the heathers are in bloom.

Use drifts The great secret of growing heathers effectively is to arrange the plants in big drifts. Plant them about a foot apart and then let them spread. Unless the bed is small, plant at least three or four specimens of one variety or colour in a group and, if possible, have half a dozen. There are many types to choose from. Arrange for the various colours to 'flow' into one another and 'flow' past one another side by side. I am thinking of half a dozen plants in a drift, with, for example, a variety of *Erica carnea*, such as King George (a dark red) next to the beautiful white Springwood, and on the other side perhaps a lovely rose pink Winter Beauty. It is surprising what patterns you can make and yet give the idea of naturalness.

WINTER FLOWERERS

In the model gardens at Arkley Manor, the winter flowering heaths are particularly admired. Many of them do not grow more than 6 ins high and with a number of varieties the display runs from late autumn to late in the following spring. Queen Mary flowers in October, Winter Beauty from November to December, the Queen of Spain in January, Pink Beauty and Ruby Glow in February followed by Springwood White. The latter is a prostrate type and makes an excellent edging.

The Mediterranean heaths are useful too and in fact one of the *Erica darleyensis* starts flowering about the middle of October and blooms as a rule until the end of February. Some of the Mediterranean heathers are low growing and flower in the spring. Others are upright and may grow to 5 or 6 ft so should be planted towards the back of the border. As a contrast there is *Erica mediterranea hibernica* Brightness growing about 2 ft high and *Erica mediterranea glauca*, a pale pink with metallic green leaves.

For damper spots For the damper spots in the garden *Erica tetralix* is used because it puts up best with winter conditions. There is also an *E. t. rubra* with wine-red flowers and *E. t. alba* – a pure white.

DWARF TYPES

For dwarf heathers much can be said for *Calluna vulgaris foxii*, which grows to about 3 in and does well for edging. A variety called Pompon is a little more upright, and its sister Ann, which has pretty silvery foliage, grows to 4 in in height. In addition, you can plant *Erica cinerea pygmaea* which bears pink flowers on stems about 3 in high. Therefore, even with a very small garden you can have these baby heathers and make a tiny plot interesting.

THE DORSET AND CORNISH TYPES

Those who know Cornwall and Dorset must know *Erica ciliaris* with its quite large flowers. There is Mrs C. H. Gill, a free flowering clear red and Stoborough, a beautiful white. *Erica cinerea* is really the British fern heather. There is *alba*, a white, *coccinea*, a dark crimson, and *Rosea*, a sturdy pink. With *Erica cinerea atropurpurea* you have a plant which is free-flowering, grows to 8 ins and is one of the best summer heaths. Don't forget the Cornish heathers: *Erica vagans rubra*, a deep rosy red, and the variety St. Keverne, a bright rose-pink which grows 2 ft tall.

Planting The tree heaths will have to be planted 3 or 4 ft apart for they take up a fair amount of room in the long run. The dwarf types can be put in 9 in apart, the medium-sized varieties 1 ft and the stronger growing varieties 18 in apart.

Make a hole with a trowel large enough to take the ball of soil from the pot in which the plants are growing. They usually arrive in cardboard or peat pots. Once the ball has been knocked out of the pot, put your fingers up among the basal roots and spread them out a little. They thus get going more quickly in the soil. Plant really firmly, pressing the soil in well around the little plant.

Continue planting the bed in groups and drifts as has already been described and then see that the surface of the soil in the bed is firm and level. Now cover the soil all over with medium-grade sedge peat one inch deep.

CHOOSING THE BEST HEATHERS

Name	Description	Time of flowering
Tree heathers		
Tree heathers have a long flowering period. Plant in groups to get the best effect.		
Erica arborea	Pale green foliage; white scented flowers. 5–6 ft.	March–April
Erica australis	Free flowering bright pink flowers. 4–6 ft.	March–May
Erica lusitanica	Long flowering period. Buds pink, opening white. 5–6 ft.	December–April
Erica veitchii	Sweetly scented; white. 5–6 ft.	April–May
Carnea varieties (winter flowers)		
These dwarf heathers are the first to bring colour to the garden in the cold months of January and February. They may be planted in bold groups. They do not mind a moderately limy soil.		
Erica carnea	Flesh pink, wonderful massing. 6 in.	December–April
Erica c. C. J. Backhouse	Pale pink. 6 in.	April–May
Erica c. King George	Deep rose-pink. 6 in.	January–April
Erica c. Praecox Rubra	Early red. 6 in.	November–March
Erica c. Prince of Wales	Pale pink, quite distinct. 6 in.	February–April
Erica c. Queen Mary	Rich pink. 6 in.	December–February
Erica c. Ruby Glow	Rich cerise. 8 in.	March–April
Erica c. Springwood Pink	The same free habit. 6 in.	February–April

Erica c. Springwood White	Free flowering, large white flowers 6 in.	February–April
Erica c. Vivellii	Rich carmine; foliage bronze-red, 6 in.	January–April
Erica c. Winter Beauty	Pink. 6 in.	January–April

Ciliaris varieties (the Dorset Heath)

Erica ciliaris	Large purple-red bells. 2 ft.	July–September
Erica ciliaris aurea	Golden foliage with pink flowers.	July–September
Erica c. Mrs. C. H. Gill	Clear red, very free. 1 ft.	July–September
Erica c. Stoborough	White flowered. 18 in.	July–September

Cinerea varieties

These provide a display from June onwards. Use them in full sun. They will not tolerate lime.

Erica cinerea	Long spikes of rosy-purple flowers. 1 ft.	June–October
Erica cinerea alba major	Terminate clusters of flowers. 9 in.	June–September
Erica cinerea atro-sanguinea (Smith's variety)	Free flowering red variety. 8 in.	August–October
Erica cinerea atro-sanguinea (Reuthes variety)	Similar to E. coccinea, but later. 6 in.	July–October
Erica cinerea coccinea	Dwarf, intense dark crimson. 4 in.	June–September
Erica cinerea C. G. Best	Vivid pink; very good 1 ft.	June–October
Erica cinerea Domino	Ebony sepals and stalks; white flowers 9 in.	June–September

Name	Description	Time of flowering
Erica cinerea Eden Valley	Lilac-pink flowers fading to white. 6 in.	June–September
Erica cinerea Golden Drop	Golden in summer, reddy-brown in winter.	
Erica cinerea Golden Hue	Golden foliage; pink flowers. 8 in.	June–September
Erica cinerea Hookstone White	Long spikes of large white flowers. 9 in.	June–October
Erica cinerea G. Osmond	Pale purple. 1 ft.	June–September
Erica cinerea Lady Skelton	Rich crimson. 6 in.	June September
Erica cinerea P. S. Patrick	Rich purple. 1 in.	June–October
Erica cinerea pygmaea	Pink flowers. 6 in.	June–September
Erica cinerea rosea	Compact in habit; rose-pink flowers. 6 in.	June–October
Erica cinerea rosea Knaphill variety	Deeper than above. 6 in.	June–October
Erica cinerea Rose Queen	Long sprays of pale rose flowers. 1 ft.	June–October
Erica cinerea Sandpit Hill	Rose-pink turning to deep red. 9 in.	June–September

Hybrids

These plants are crosses between the species.

Name	Description	Time of flowering
Erica hybrida darleyensis	Purple-rose flowers. 18 in.	December–April
Erica hybrida Arthur Johnson	Deeper coloured flowers. 1 ft.	December–April
Erica hybrida George Randall	A deeper form of E. Darleyensis. 1 ft.	December–April
Erica hybrida Gwavas	Young shoots tipped with yellow flowers; pink. 1 ft.	June–October
Erica hybrida H. Maxwell	Bright pink flowers. A moist position. 1 ft.	June–September

Name	Description	Flowering
Erica hybrida stuartii	An unusual heather with pink flowers.	July–October
Erica hybrida watsonii	Large pink flowers. 6 in.	July–October
Erica hybrida williamsii	Clear pink flowers in profusion; shoots tipped with gold.	June–September

Mediterranea

Early spring flowering, bushy, upright habit. Masses of flowers.

Name	Description	Flowering
Erica mediterranea	Good free flowering, 4–5 ft.	February–April
Erica mediterranea hibernica	Pale pink. 3–4 ft.	March–April
Erica mediterranea hibernica Brightness	Dwarf habit. Red flowers and bronze buds. 2 ft.	March–April
Erica mediterranea W. T. Rackliff	The best white. 2 ft.	April–February
Erica mediterranea silberschmelze (Silverbells)	A white Darleyensis. 1 ft.	January–April
Erica mediterranea Rosea superba	Clear pink.	March–April
Erica mediterranea superba	Large pink flowers. 5 ft.	March–April
Erica mediterranea stricta	Makes a neat rounded bush. 4–5 ft. Pink. Does not mind limy soil.	June–September

Name	Description	Time of flowering
Tetralix types		
These are happy in moist positions.		
Erica tetralix	Rosy-purple. 6 in.	June–September
Erica tetralix alba mollis	Has white flowers and silver foliage. 6 in.	June–September
Erica tetralix Con. Underwood	Richest deep crimson. 9 in.	June–September
Erica tetralix Ken Underwood	Large cerise flowers. 1 ft.	June–September
Erica tetralix L. E. Underwood	Soft apricot-flushed terra cotta. 6 in.	June–September
Erica tetralix Mary Grace	Pink; silver foliage. 6 in.	June–September
Erica tetralix praegeri	Soft mauve flowers; upright stems. 6 in.	June–September
Vagans		
Heathers of compact habit. The whole plant is covered with flowers. They give a wonderful display.		
Erica vagans George Underwood	Pink flowers. Strong-growing and compact.	July–October
Erica vagans Hookstone rosea	Clear pink.	July–October
Erica vagans kevernensis alba	Close heads, small white flowers. 1 ft.	July–September
Erica vagans Mrs. D. F. Maxwell	Deep cerise. 2 ft.	July–October
Erica vagans nana	Dwarf with creamy white flowers. 6 in.	July–October
Erica vagans Pyrenees Pink	Neat and compact pink flowers. 9 in.	August–October
Erica vagans rubra	Deep purple-red flowers. 1 ft.	July–October
Erica vagans St. Keverne	Bright rose-pink flowers. 1 ft.	July–October
Erica vagans vagans cream	A bright creamy white, red anthers. 2 ft.	July–October

Vulgaris (Calluna Vulgaris types)

A collection of varieties suitable for the wild garden.

Erica vulgaris alba	The white heather of Scotland. 2 ft.	July–September
Erica vulgaris alba plena	Fully double white flowers. 18 in.	August–October
Erica vulgaris alportii	Crimson flowers on upright stalks. 2 ft.	July–October
Erica vulgaris August Beauty	Free flowering, white. 1 ft.	August–September
Erica vulgaris aurea	Deep golden, changing to an intense red. 1 ft.	August–October
Erica vulgaris County Wicklow	Double pink flowers. 9 in.	August–September
Erica vulgaris cuprea	Copper foliage; purple flowers.	August–October
Erica vulgaris C. W. Nix	Bright crimson flowers on long spikes.	August–October
Erica vulgaris E. Hoare	Matted foliage; bright crimson flowers. 18 in.	August–October
Erica vulgaris elata alba	White flowers; feathery stems.	August–October
Erica vulgaris flore pleno	A double pink. 2 ft.	August–October
Erica vulgaris foxii nana	Deep green mound; purple flowers. 3 in.	August–September
Erica vulgaris Goldsworth Crimson	Latest of the crimsons to flower. 2 ft.	October–November
Erica vulgaris Goldsworth Crimson Variegated		September
Erica vulgaris H. E. Beale	10 in spikes of double rose-pink flowers. 2 ft.	September–October
Erica vulgaris hirsuta compacta	Miniature silver foliage turning red in winter 3 in.	August–September
Erica vulgaris hyemalis	Mauve flowers almost the last to flower.	September–October
Erica vulgaris J. F. Hamilton	One of the best doubles. Pink. 9 in.	September–October

Name	Description	Time of flowering
Erica vulgaris Mrs. Ronald Gray	Prostrate with purple flowers. 3 in.	August–September
Erica vulgaris Mullion	Compact type with deep pink flowers on close growing spikes.	September–October
Erica vulgaris nana compacta	Flowers freely. 3 in.	August–September
Erica vulgaris rigida prostrata	Dwarf, growing white; golden foliage with pink flowers. 2 ft.	August–September
Erica vulgaris serlei	A fine, late flowering white. 2 ft.	September–October
Erica vulgaris serlei grandiflora rubra	Late purple. 3 ft.	September–November
Erica vulgaris tenuis Goldsworth	Crimson variety, beautifully variegated.	July–October
Erica vulgaris Tib	Rich double pink flowers; free-flowering.	August–September
Erica vulgaris tricolorfolia	Foliage green, pink and yellow. Very effective. 2 ft.	August–September
Erica vulgaris underwoodii	Silver-pink buds which fade and turn white. 1 ft.	July–October

Menziesia (Daboecia types)

Erica menziesia prolifolia	Purple-pink flowers; upright stems. 2 ft.	June–October
Erica menziesia praegeraea	Cerise flowers on upright stems. 2 ft.	June–October
Erica menziesia purpurea	Flowers bright purple; foliage dark green, 2 ft.	June–October
Erica menziesia atro purpurea	Rich purple bells. 2 ft.	June
Erica menziesia Hookstone Purple	Flowers large, strong grower, 3 ft.	June–October
Erica menziesia bruckenthalia spidulifolia	A small plant; pink flowers. 9 in.	June–July

12 A simple iris garden

One of the simplest and most easy to manage flower beds you can have in the garden is one devoted to the bearded irises. These plants are particularly suitable for gardens in Kent, Buckinghamshire and the like where the soil is limy. However, gardeners of slightly acid soils should not be deterred, for the best irises seem to accommodate themselves anywhere. There is no need to carry out any special preparation of the soil: quite shallow forking will do, and the plants will be just as happy in a sloping bed as in one that is flat.

Once planted, the iris needs hardly any attention. The flowering stems will be cut back when blooming time is over. The leaves will be cut back by half in July to tidy the bed and also to discourage the appearance of Leaf spot disease. The bed will be mulched with dark brown powdery compost or sedge peat one inch deep as in the case of the flower border, and so there will be no hoeing or weeding to do.

Sacheverell Sitwell said, 'The iris has absolute as well as objective beauty for it can stay dumb, or speak to us in many languages'.

Bearded irises have come to us from the Orient, Kashmir, China and Japan, from Sicily and Bruges as well as from Palestine and Persia. In many ways the greatest developments of the iris are perhaps yet to come. Advances have been made in the last decade, but because of development in the scentific breeding of the bearded iris in recent years, we may see some wonderful changes in colour and form before long.

Those who come to the Open Days of *The Good Gardeners' Association* at Arkley Manor in May and June invariably make their way first to the irises. Growing in the sun, the iris bank is aglow with colour. Irises en masse are at their best. The iris is beloved because, although tall and bold, it needs no support, and the bluey-green foliage is attractive in the spring before it flowers, and in summer after the flowering.

Bearded irises are basically lime lovers, so if you have acid soil apply carbonate of lime, about half a pound to the square yard or even more, when the bed is being forked over. Irises revel in phosphates, so bone meal can be given at the same time at 4 to 5 ozs to the square yard. This acts slowly but surely.

There are many varieties and colours so those who want an iris garden for the first time will do well not only to consult a nurseryman's catalogue but also to go to a nursery garden or garden centre to see the varieties flowering.

Ordering As irises should be planted as soon as possible after flowering, the nurseryman can be given the order on the spot and be persuaded to deliver in a few weeks. Aim to plant in late June. Each plant should consist of two or three sword-like leaves interleaved with each other, a thick root portion (about two fingers thick and known as rhizome) from which extend a number of roots. The roots are planted and the rhizome sits on the top soil, benefiting from the sun.

The fan of leaves, as it is called, may be only 6 or 7 ins high. Some nurserymen send a larger plant consisting of say two fans but this is rare.

Washing Wash, preferably under a running tap, the rhizomes and the roots so that all alien soil is removed before planting in your good ground. Next put the rhizomes in a zinc bath or tub of water, in the shade, leaving for the best part of the day. This ensures that the foliage is rugged and fresh before planting.

Planting Plant the roots shallowly and firmly and if the plant is very dry put an overhead water sprinkler in position over the bed to supply a few hours of artificial rain.

Plant irises 18 ins apart, so that the rhizomes are exposed
to the sun, and give them room to spread; then you can
leave them undisturbed for perhaps five years. After that
the rhizomes will be so large they will have to be dug up
for replanting. The oldest ones should be thrown away
on the compost heap.

For the best effect plant in drifts of five or six rhizomes
of a variety. Follow the general advice in Chapter 5: have
the blues drifting into the mauves, the whites and the light
blues separating the almost-reds from the chocolates and
plan the border to make the most colour blends and con-
trasts. Label all the varieties and, for permanence, use
indestructible plastic labels which stand about 3 in
above the ground. These the author uses right through
his garden because they save time. Wooden labels
painted, even with Indian ink, constantly need renewing.

Mulching After planting (say at the end of June) put a
half-inch layer of medium-grade sedge peat or home-made
compost over the bed. The idea is not to bury the rhizomes
but to smother the annual weeds, for an iris garden must
be kept free of weeds all the time. The secret is to keep
the rhizomes dry and sun-baked, so never put the sedge
peat on the actual rhizomes themselves or as deeply on the
bed so as to bury them. Add more peat in the autumn if
the worms pull in some of it. Keep the peat at about the
1 inch depth for a weedless, trouble free border.

Feeding In early October apply a fish fertilizer or a seaweed manure at 3 ozs to the square yard and allow this
to work through the sedge peat naturally. If the leaves
were not cut back by about half in July or August do this
before applying the manure. For those who like specific
instructions, the foliage must be cut within 6 ins of soil
in late September.

On poor soil a second similar application of fish or seaweed manure must be given early in April. If the no-work
gardener concentrates on growing varieties which do not
grow too tall and which do not have large heavy flowers,

supporting and staking will not be necessary. The only work that does help to ensure perfection is the removal of the dying flowers every two or three days.

For those willing to devote a bed to a plant that looks at its best for two months of the year or so, the iris has much to recommend it.

Varieties There are hundreds to choose from – but here are some extra beautiful kinds which need the minimum of work. Buy one of each to start wth if you wish and then propogate by division in three or four years time and plant a large area. Splitting is easy. The only secret is to keep the younger portions and throw away the older rhizomes.

Good, easy to grow varieties (Iris germanica)

Name	Description	Height
Aline	Very strongly scented; pure azure blue.	3 ft
Amethyst Flame	Immense flower, very elegant A tinted blend of light violet and heliotrope.	3 ft 2 in
Bang	Magnificent red. Large blooms between cedar and indian red.	3 ft
Black Swan	Near black – has matching wide bronze tipped beard.	3 ft
Blue Rhythm	Mid cornflower-blue.	$3\frac{1}{2}$ ft
Buttermere	A fine yellow.	3 ft
Confetti	Pink-hued.	3 ft (over)
Craithie	Bright: pure seashcll-pink with touch of grey at haft.	3 ft
Deep Black	Very dark purple.	3 ft
Ethereal Sky	Pale blue-shaded turquoise.	3 ft
Fascination	Brilliant lilac-pink; scented.	4 ft
Gilded Minaret	Metallic gold.	3 ft 10 in
Great Day	Fine deep red.	3 ft
Happy Birthday	Light pink with bright orange-red beard.	3 ft
Immortal Hour	Pure white; free flowering.	3 ft 2 in

Name	*Description*	*Height*
June Meredith	One of the pinkest of irises with tangerine beard.	3 ft
Licorice Stick	A deep blue-black including the beard.	3 ft 4 in
Lockwood	Brilliant coppery-brown blend.	$3\frac{1}{2}$ ft
Marion Hamilton	Apricot; large flowered.	3 ft
Marshglow	Brick red; good shape.	2 ft 11 in
Memories	Very fine clear pink with red beard.	3 ft
Pale Primrose	Primrose yellow; ruffled form.	3 ft
Party Dress	Ruffled flamingo-pink flowers with tangerine beard.	3 ft
Ranger	Deep crimson red; free flowering.	3 ft
Rosemary Lane	Orchid pink.	3 ft
Sable	Blackish-violet with a claret tone. Blue-bearded.	$3\frac{1}{2}$ ft
Shepherds	Strong pink with tinge of yellow about the haft.	3 ft 2 in
Staten Island	Bright gold, port wine red falls with sharp gold margins.	3 ft
Tall Chief	Bright brazil-red and carmine.	3 ft 2 in
Trophy	Mauvy-blue, large flowered.	2 ft 6 in
Tyrian Prince	Gorgeous red-purple.	3 ft 2 in
Varsity Blue	A Blue-bearded cobalt blue.	2 ft 10 in
Wheal Prosperous	Deep lavender; excellent shape.	3 ft 6 in
Wheal Vor	Royal purple with navy blue beard.	3 ft
Wicca	A fine navy blue.	2 ft 4 in

Dwarf bearded Irises

Acolyte	Dark violet including the beard.	10 in
Blazon Day	Yellow with slightly lighter standards.	10 in
Blue Beard	White and olive bicolour.	9 in
Double Lament	Deep violet with orange beard.	11 in

Name	Description	Height
Greenspot	Pure white with large bright green spot on each fall.	10 in
Happy Thought	Soft sulphur yellow.	10 in
Lenna M.	Apricot-pink with deeper falls and white beard red-tipped.	10 in
Lilliwhite	Pure white with ruffled near horizontal falls.	10 in
Moonspinner	Palest lemon changing to white with warm white falls.	10 in
Path of Gold	Fine golden-yellow pumila.	6 in
Sissinghurst	Dark purple with bronze beard.	11 in
Tangerose	Rose-red with dark flush on talls and a tangerine beard.	
Velvet Caper	Very deep purple with deep purple beard.	12 i.

13 A weedless Alpine scree

A man-made scree garden is quite a novelty to some people. Yet it is ideal because it is composed almost entirely of stones of various sizes and weeds won't grow in it! The scree is no home for chickweed, groundsel, Shepherd's Purse, annual nettles and the like, all of which prefer soil. Take the trouble to prepare a scree and you will be able to grow successfully and easily all the plants I have listed at the end of the chapter, without any hoeing, weeding or forking.

The scree is a wonderful garden. I discovered it unexpectedly when visiting a friend who lived in the Wirral Peninsula of Cheshire. This scree garden was so attractive and yet it needed no looking after. I wanted to tell everyone about it and as I was then the Gardening Editor of the B.B.C. (North Region) I took the opportunity of talking about it over the air.

Readers who have been to Wastwater may remember the sight of the screes as they slide down Sca Fell. The idea is to have man-made screes in one's garden which cannot, of course, appear to slide down a mountainside, but which can be made as a special bed in some convenient spot. In the garden you will not need to use big boulders but just concentrate on thousands of stones. It cannot be said to be minimum-work gardening to start with because you will have to do a fair amount of preparation. Having dug out the bed to be used for a scree to the depth of 18 ins or so, bigger stones are put into the bottom, the smaller stones above, still smaller stones above this until the surface is covered with tiny little stones and chippings in which the plants grow.

You can use any stones you like – granite, sandstones, millstone grit and even flint. They have all been successfully used for this purpose. Include a proportion of sedge peat and soil with the smaller stones that you use for the top 2 ins. You need four parts of stones to one part of really fibrous soil and one part of sedge peat. Such a scree garden may have to be raised. It is always a good thing anyway to have the beds about 5 ins higher than the path, for drainage purposes.

The advantage of a scree garden is that you can grow many kinds of difficult Alpine plants which on ordinary soil would not have a chance. It would be unwise to try to suggest the names of *all* the plants that could be grown in the scree. The best plan is to go to a good Alpine nurseryman and make a choice of the plants whose shape and colour attract you. It is always a good thing to see plants before trying to grow them. To start with, concentrate on the more easy-to-grow types such as dwarf phloxes and aubretias, and then graduate to plants like edelweiss. Incidentally, this prefers a limestone scree, so when covering the top of the scree garden with little stones, be sure to use some limestone chippings and you will be able to grow this plant.

It is difficult to make a choice of plants out of the huge selection available. There are many different types of primula for instance, and there are beautiful little plants like *Zauschneria californica* and *Asperula arcadiensis*. Take note that it is important to buy plants with a really good root system, and once again, see to it that the plants are planted in drifts and not in straight lines. There should be a little group here, a drift of two or three there, and so on. The planting must look natural.

Here is a selection of plants that I have found to grow well in a scree.

Selected Alpines

Name	Description	Time of flowering
Agathaea coelestis	Blue	June–September
Androsace (all species)	Pink and white	April–October
Anemone vernalis	Silver-white	March

Name	Description	Time of flowering
Aquilegia ecalcarata	Brown-purple	May–June
Calandrina umbellata	Magenta	July–September
Calceolaria darwinii	Yellow and red	July
Chrysanthemum mawii	Pink	June–September
Dianthus Peris allwoodii	Pink	June–September
Dianthus alpinus	Deep rose	June–July
Dianthus microlepis	Pink	June–July
Draba aizoides	Golden	March–April
Erigeron leiomerus	Violet	June
Erythraea diffusa	Pink	June
Gentiana farreri	Light blue	September–October
Geranium argenteum	Rose-pink	June
Hypericum empetrifolium	Yellow	June–September
Hypsella longiflora	Purplish pink	June–September
Linaria alpina	Purple and pink	May–July
Origanum dictamnus	Rose-purple	June–September
Papaver alpina	Various	May–September
Phlox adsurgens	Shell pink	May
Phlox douglasii	Lilac	May
Potentilla nitida	Pink	June–July
Ranunculus alpestris	White	June–July
Raoulia (all species)	White; silver foliage	July
Scutellaria japonica	Dark violet	July
Shortia uniflora	Pink	June–August
Silene acaulis	Pink	June–August
Statice bellidifolia	Mauve	July–September
Thymus serpyllum coccineus	Red	July–August
Verbena chamaedrifolia	Scarlet	June–September
Veronica bidwillii minor	White	June

14 Cut-work culture for vegetables

There are two ways of running the vegetable garden in order to save time and labour. The first is to plan all the rows so as to fit a small rotary cultivator, or to put it another way – so that the rotary cultivator goes down in between the rows to control weeds perfectly. At Arkley Manor, for instance, all the rows are either 18 ins apart or 3 ft apart. Thus the baby Rotovator goes down the 18 inch rows once, and down the 3 ft apart rows twice.

The second method is more suitable for small vegetable plots. In this case the whole of the garden is covered with medium-grade sedge peat one inch deep. The small seeds are then sown in the sedge peat about half an inch deep and, in the case of bigger seeds like peas and beans, the sedge peat is moved to one side of the line and a drill is made with a hoe 2 ins deep and the seeds sown. After sowing and covering over, the peat is raked back.

The alternative is to sow all the seeds first and then, when the plants are through, apply the sedge peat so as to prevent any annual weeds from growing.

In both cases properly rotted 'powdery' compost may be used instead of the sedge peat and this is of course, cheaper, because it is made in the garden. In both cases, however, if the weather is very dry, the top dressing of organic matter must be kept moist. Seeds won't germinate in very dry peat.

In the large demonstration allotment of *The Good Gardeners' Association* at Arkley, the compost is put all over the ground at about 1 inch deep and is then raked in to the depth of one inch or so by a long tined rake like the tines of a fork bent to an angle of 90 degrees. The seeds are sown in this, usually with an automatic seed sower like 'The Bean'. The hopper is filled with the seed and a special dix is fitted so that the holes in it are commensurate with the size of the seeds. The machine can be set so that the seeds are sown thickly or thinly. It has two wheels and a little iron shoe. This makes the necessary drill ahead of the operator. This machine has only to be pushed along, and the seeds automatically drop into the soil in the right places. It only takes a few minutes to learn how to use it skilfully.

Whether the sowing is done by hand or machine, it is an advantage to make the rows long. Short rows are a nuisance. Eliminate all paths in the vegetable garden and it should be possible to cultivate and sow with the minimum of stopping and starting.

This means, alas, that there is a certain amount of hand hoeing to be done in the summer. However, by not having to do any digging and any forking a tremendous amount of labour is saved. Bastard trenching or deep digging are both out and in fact the mini-work gardener can count on excellent results without backbreaking work.

In either the peat (or compost) mulching method or the rotovation method, fish or seaweed manure should be used at 4 ozs to the square yard in the spring just before the seeds are put in. It need only be put on the top of the compost before rotovation or on the soil before the sedge peat is applied. Only a few weeds will occur with this method.

VEGETABLES WITHOUT DIGGING

Of course, the ground is not dug in the autumn or early winter. Instead, in the late autumn, the whole of the area where the seeds are to be sown is covered with properly made compost. This must be fully decomposed, powdery fine and dark brown in colour and if it isn't fine enough it must be sifted through a $\frac{1}{2}$ inch riddle. Those who cannot or do not want to make compost may use medium grade sedge peat instead. Apply at least three two gallon pailfuls of either to the square yard and evenly spread it all over the area.

In the spring when seed sowing time comes round, the soil should be raked with a deep tined rake. Thus the powdery compost is incorporated into the top inch or so of soil. The seed can then be sown in a mixture of soil and compost. With a pointed stick or the corner of a hoe scratch out a little V-shaped drill and sow the seeds thinly in this. Then tread the soil and compost back again. Larger seeds, like those of peas and beans, may be sown a little deeper at the right distance apart and should be well watered afterwards.

Those who prefer can put the compost in position in late March. It should then be thoroughly soaked with water before sowing and will retain the moisture. It should be possible as a result to sow seeds even though the ground below may appear to be dry.

When the peas and beans are harvested after growing under such conditions, cut down the stems to soil level. Do not dig up the roots. In this way the nitrogen nodules formed on these roots are left in the soil for the following year's crop, which should preferably be some member of the cabbage family.

When harvesting root crops, however, it is not possible to leave the ground exactly as it was originally because the roots have, as a rule, to be forked out. You can, however, rake back the compost, leaving the top as level as possible. Afterwards, however, please roll or tread well. Another layer of fine compost will have to be applied all over the top of the ground before the next batch of seeds is sown.

Under this method of culture, the planting out of seedlings is simple. The compost or sedge peat is put on the ground as a surface dressing in the normal way. A hole is then made with a dibber or trowel and the plant is put into position and firmed. The compost or sedge peat remains on top and helps to smother weeds.

This method, of course, saves much digging and forking – but it does entail making large quantities of compost or buying adequate amounts of sedge peat instead. Some gardeners have suggested that labour is not saved, because of the work concerned with making and trans- porting the compost. This is not so, because compost has to be made month after month even by those who still cling to digging methods!

Those who want to save time, and space on compost making should use medium grade sedge peat. When the Horticultural Training Centre was at Thaxted special no-digging beds were laid out for growing vegetables and by using sedge peat entirely as a top dressing and feeding the rows of plants through the peat with a product like Marinure. Lettuces, peas, spinach, radishes, turnips and French beans were all grown successfully by this no-dig- ging method for over five years and experiments proved to be a success.

Sedge peat usually arrives in bags – it is therefore easy to apply. It is weed and disease free and, when spread to the depth of an inch or so, it smothers the weeds and makes a grand medium in which to sow seeds or plant plants.

A few simple rules for no diggers:

1 Do not dig the ground but start as far as possible with it being fairly level.

2 Use well rotted, finely divided compost and apply this evenly all over the surface, preferably late in October.

3 Sowing of seeds: if they are tiny, sow in the soil mixed with the compost; if large, sow a little deeper.

4 Those who have not got enough compost in their first year can use sedge peat instead. This may have to be moistened if it is used in the spring but it can be put on dry in October.

5 Each year a further dressing of compost should be applied on the top if the worms have pulled some in, and every time a new crop is sown or planted it may be necessary to put on a little more compost.

6 In addition to the compost or sedge peat, a fish or seaweed fertilizer should be used at 3 to 4 ozs to the square yard.

Exceptions to the rule:

1 Jerusalem artichokes have to be planted with a dibber 3 or 4 ins deep and then compost filled in over the top.

2 Outdoor cucumbers: just make a hole in the ground with a trowel and put in the plants: then put sedge peat all around.

3 Leeks: make dibber holes 6 ins deep, pop the plants in and add water. As the plants grow, put more compost or sedge peat along the sides.

4 Potatoes: scrape out a furrow with a draw hoe 3 ins wide and 2 ins deep. Put the potatoes in the bottom at the right distances apart and cover with the compost instead of soil, or make little holes like 'nests' and put one tuber in each nest at the right distance apart.

5 Rhubarb: put in the plants and then cover the soil with compost or sedge peat.

6 Tomatoes: plant with a trowel and make firm; then put a 2 inch mulch of sedge peat all over the ground.

SOWING SEEDS

It certainly helps a man to enjoy good gardening if he makes up his mind to spend wisely on 'pedigree' seeds. There have been many disappointments in the past in gardens, owing to amateurs buying poor seeds thinking that they are saving money. Go to a reliable seedsman and send in the order early, for the rule is often 'first come first served'.

Remember also that there are good strains of particular varieties and it pays to get them. Take for instance the variety of onion, Ailsa Craig. It is possible to get some strains of this onion that will produce very large bulbs, while there are inferior strains that will never crop as heavily. If any readers have difficulties with seed purchases, the author will be happy to help.

Choose a good day for the work. The planting out of Brassicas and the like should be done in showery weather if possible, and shallow hoeing be carried out during a sunny period. If it is necessary to run over the soil with a barrow in the winter then the least damage to the structure of the soil will occur if you do the work when the earth is frozen. It is always advantageous to treat the soil properly, and every gardener should be prepared to delay any job for a week or so until the weather is right. No one who does this ever loses by it.

Having made a drill in which to sow the seeds, do not just sprinkle them along evenly from one end to the other, or waste may occur. Adopt what is known as 'station' sowing. This means that three seeds are dropped every so many inches along the drill. For lettuces, it would be every 8 ins, for parsnips every 5 ins, and so on. If this is done there will be less thinning out later. The gardener will in fact only have to thin to one 'per station' if the seeds all grow, instead of having to pull out hundreds of seedlings that are of no value.

Never mind kneeling when sowing. Somehow, gardeners always imagine they ought to work bending their back almost double. Kneeling is a comfortable posture, and if the rows are straddled the gardener can crawl along the drills and do the work with the minimum exertion and maximum efficiency. By this method also the worker has two hands to work with, and so the job becomes simple – and expeditious.

Some friends of the author provide themselves with knee-pads while kneeling, made of 'foam' rubber or old carpets. Others use sacks tied round their knees! It is certainly not infra dig to work kneeling. Market gardeners in fact employ men who are called 'crawlers'. These work at thinning and hoeing on their knees with short onion hoes, and never bend down at all.

SAVING LABOUR WITH DIFFERENT TYPES OF VEGETABLES

With peas, stick to the dwarf varieties. These can be sown

much closer between the rows than the taller varieties; there is thus little difference in the total yield per square yard. Choose varieties that are no taller than 18 ins. Thus they are 18 ins high, the rows need to be 18 ins apart and this fits into the standardized scheme.

With broad beans, too, choose the smaller types. A good variety is *The Sutton*. With runner beans, to save the bother of providing tall sticks up which plants are to grow, have them on what is called 'the flat'. That is to say, sow the seeds in rows 3 ft apart and use a variety called Hammonds' Dwarf. The plants of this variety keep low and within bounds – somewhat like french beans.

Do not try to grow a vegetable such as celery, because it needs trenches and a lot of work, the exception being the American Green celery. Those who fancy this type should plant out the seedlings a foot apart. In my opinion green celery is just as delicious as white celery. It doesn't look as nice – that is all!

Normally the 'station' sowing method should be used for all root crops so that no thinning has to be done, but with carrots sow thinly in continuous rows. It helps if the seed is mixed with about three times its bulk of dusty peat or sand. Do not attempt to thin out roots: just pull them as required and thus thin them as they are needed. This is a particularly useful method, of course, when sowings are made in July for pulling in the autumn.

With beetroot sow at stations 3 ins apart. Thin down to one per station three weeks later and when the roots are the size of golf balls thin out every other one. Thus an early crop is achieved as well as a late one.

For the cabbage family – the Brussels sprouts, cauli-flowers, savoys, cabbages and so on – the simplest method is to sow the seed where the plants are to grow. This means that the ground is taken up much earlier than it would be if you sowed the seeds first in beds and then transplanted later, but it is a great saving in labour and time. Without transplanting, the cabbages, brussels sprouts and the like will do far better.

PLATE 8. The author in the unusual vegetable garden at Arkley Manor.

The leek is usually grown in trenches, but to save time it can easily be planted with the ordinary dibber. At Arkley excellent leeks are produced by having the rows only 8 ins apart and the plants only 6 ins apart in the rows. Dibble holes are made 6 ins deep; one plant is dropped into the bottom of each; a little water is poured into the hole, and nothing more is done.

The leeks gradually swell and fill up the dibble hole. No earthing up has to be done later on, and they blanch quite well on their own. This is the best way to grow leeks if the maximum production is desired with the minimum of work. Few people today want the huge specimens that our grandfathers seemed to delight in.

With marrows, sow two seeds where the plants are to grow, and put an upturned jam-jar over the top to protect and give extra heat. The moment the marrow plant or plants have started to grow and are filling the glass, the jam-jar can be removed. If both seeds grow, one should be pulled out carefully. This sowing is done about the beginning of May.

With onions there is no need to thin out the seedlings if the seed is sown thinly enough in the first place. $\frac{1}{2}$ oz of seed is needed to a 60 yard row. The seedlings will seem thick when they first come up, but if they are left a heavy crop of small bulbs will result. Of course, those who are exhibitors and want to win at shows should thin and feed and do all sorts of things, but for ordinary household use the smaller bulbs are delicious.

It is difficult to suggest a mini-work way of growing potatoes, but there is one known as the 'lazy man's method' or 'lazy banks' in Ireland. This consists of putting the potatoes on the surface of the ground and then digging the soil out shallowly on either side in order to cover the tubers. This ensures a slight ridge. Then, when the potatoes grow up, more soil is dug if necessary to do what is called 'earthing up'. The system was devised in Ireland on soil where the water-level is near the surface.

Another simple method, known as the 'flat' system, is used where the land dries out quickly. A hole is dug for each potato along a row; the soil from hole 2 is used to cover up the potato put into hole 1, the soil from hole 3 covers the potato in hole 2 and so on. The holes are fairly shallow, and the plan used to be for one person to dig the hole and a boy to put the potato in position. In the old days a man used to plant an acre of land a day by this method.

The third way which some Fellows of *The Good Gardeners' Association* adopt is to put the 'seed' potatoes on the surface of the ground or in a depression like a nest an inch deep – and then to cover them with old semi-rotten straw, or half rotted compost. The potatoes then grow with this coverage and are very easy to harvest.

As to varieties, the author can recommend Foremost as an early, not for its flavour but because it is almost immune to the potato blight disease. The other kinds that are high-resisting would appear to be Red Skin as a second early, and Dr. Mackintosh as a late.

With tomatoes, the secret is to grow a dwarf variety like Amateur, and to plant it about 2 ft square. Cover the soil all around the plants with sedge peat to the depth of 1 inch for about 9 ins on either side. The plants of this variety do not need any de-shooting or tying up; they grow naturally on the ground and crop heavily.

Rhubarb, though used as a fruit, must be included as a vegetable. In the Arkley trial grounds some twenty-five different varieties are grown. Timperley Early is the earliest, Champagne a good mid-season kind and the Sutton a late. Buy in what are called rhubarb 'sets'. Make a hole with a trowel to plant them 3 ft apart in October. In the spring cover with straw a foot deep and there should be little more work to do. If some of the straw is pulled into the ground by the worms add some more.

The Jerusalem artichoke is another easy to grow vegetable providing it is planted where it need not be disturbed, i.e. at the bottom of the allotment or garden. Be sure to grow the variety Fuseau and plant the smooth tubers 1 ft apart in a row and 5 ins deep. Cover the row after planting with good compost 6 ins deep. Cut down the 6 ft stems in October by half, and put them on the compost heap. Fork up the artichokes as you need them for soup or as a vegetable. They are particularly easy to digest. Never replant artichokes. There are always sufficient tubers left in the ground after harvesting to ensure a heavy crop the following year.

Salsify is disease-free, pest-free and an easy vegetable to grow. Sow the seeds thinly in a drill 1 inch deep in April. If two rows are needed the next should be 9 ins away. It is easy to make one $\frac{1}{4}$ oz packet of seed sow two rows 12 ft long. Treat this root crop like carrots, only thin the plants out to 2 ins apart. The roots are white and very delicious and are said to have an 'oyster' flavour. Harvest in November as desired.

Rolo Cultivator Fellows of *The Good Gardeners'
Association* have been very satisfied with the Rolo Cultivator which can be adapted to plough very shallowly – hoe
or rake. The hoes with the rake behind produce a good tilth
with little effort. Some people use the little single plough
for making a shallow furrow in which to sow bean seeds.
It is made by a firm called Agricultural Improvements,
5, St. Andrews Road, Great Malvern, Worcs.

The plan of operation is to push the cultivator forward
to arms' length and draw back with the blades deeply
engaged. This prepares the soil and then, when hoeing,
the tool can be used at walking pace. There are various
attachments that can be used such as ridgers, hoers and
rakes.

15 The herb garden

In the gardens at Arkley Manor, will be found two herb gardens. One is a raised long shaped bed by the kitchen door in which are grown the bulk of the culinary herbs so that the cook can dash out at any moment and cut and use fresh the flavours she needs. The other is down in a semi-shady spot where herbs of all kinds grow happily; the scented ones like Bergamot as well as the types which produce seeds like the caraway, which many people like in cakes and soups.

In both cases the production is carried out on mini-work lines. Once the herbs have been planted or the seeds sown, the whole bed is covered with powdery dark compost or medium grade sedge peat an inch deep, so the annual weeds do not grow and so there is no hoeing to do. Further, the top dressing, (or mulch), keeps the moisture in the soil and the herbs grow quietly and definitely and are never checked by dry weather. The result is that the flowers and scents of the plants are enhanced, while the leaves that are used straight from the plants are succulent and delicious.

In the 3 ft wide long strip bed outside the kitchen door, the plants are set out in serried rows 1 ft and 18 ins apart, depending on their height. This is a functional border and looks what it is, with the plants, as it were, all standing at attention, waiting for the cook and her knife to remove the portions that are required. In the larger border the plants are set out to look attractive; a drift of light green feathery plant, like fennel, with a group of deep green leaved herbs like the broad leaved sage nearby to give interest. Such a bed may be planted to suit the desires and artistry of the garden owner.

As to the types of herbs I can recommend and a few brief notes on their culture the following list may prove useful:

Anis An annual growing 1 ft tall. Sow the seed in April. Thin out the plants in May to 1 ft apart. The seed itself is used by the cook.

Balm A perennial growing $2\frac{1}{2}$ ft high. Plant in May or autumn. Is easily propagated by the division of roots. The leaves are used fresh and dried.

Bush Basil Grows 8 ins high. Sow seed in April, in rows 1 ft apart and have the plants 8 ins apart in the rows. Use the leaves fresh as they have a tang of cloves about them, or dry the leaves and use in stuffing and soups.

Bergamot A perennial; plant 18 ins by 1 ft. The plants grow 3 ft high. Use the red petals of the flowers and the leaves in a salad. The flavour is strong.

Borage A decorative herb with lovely blue flowers. Sow seeds mid-April and thin out to 1 ft apart. Use the blue flowers in salads. The leaves can be used to make a cooling tea.

Chamomile A Prostrate growing plant. Plant 8 ins square and soon there will be a complete carpet. Chamomile tea is liked.

Caraway Sow seeds in the spring 1 ft apart. Cut down the plants as soon as the seeds begin to ripen. When fully dried the seeds can be stored in a jar with a tight lid.

Chervil Grows 1 ft high. Sow seed in the spring and again in July, in rows 1 ft apart and thin out to 8 ins apart. Use the leaves in salads.

Dill Sow the seed in April in rows 9 ins apart and thin out to 9 ins also. Choose a sunny spot. Use the chopped up leaves in a salad.

Fennel Sow the seeds mid-April in rows 3 ft apart and thin out to 1 ft and later to 2 ft. Use the tender stems 6 ins high and pick leaves at any time using them cut up in a salad. The leaves are feathery.

Marjoram Sever root shoots from old plants, and plant these out 1 ft apart. Do the harvesting just before the flowers open in July. Use as a flavouring for omelettes or scrambled eggs.

Mint There are many different mints. The best mint sauce is made from an equal mixture of Apple Mint and Lamb Mint. Never have a bed down longer than five years. Plant in rows 1 ft apart and 8 ins between the plants. Keep down the rust disease by burning off the tops each early October.

Parsley Sow the moss curled type shallowly as an edging plant to a rose bed, because roses and parsley love one another. Water the soil with boiling water – this helps germination. Sow in April and again in August; covering the soil with sedge peat where the parsley is growing prevents the foliage from becoming gritty.

Purslane Grow in full sun. Sow the seed Mid-May in rows 1 ft apart. Thin out to 6 ins. For succession, sow again a month later. Use the leaves in salads and sandwiches.

Sage This pleasant herb prefers a light soil and an open situation. Sow seeds in May in rows 9 ins apart and thin the seedlings out to 9 ins apart later. Use fresh leaves in salads or dry them and use in stuffings and flavourings.

Savory Grow the summer savory like parsley. Have the drills 1 ft apart and thin out the seedlings when they come up to 9 ins apart. Cut twice in the season to prevent the plants becoming woody. The rows should last six years.

Sorrel Sow seed in drills 1 ft apart – thin the seedlings out to 6 ins apart. A French sorrel is the best for salads and soups.

Tarragon Grow in poor soil choosing the French type. Buy young plants and plant in April 1 ft apart. Cut the plants in July and September. Tarragon makes an excellent sauce for fish and, of course, is the main ingredient of Tarragon vinegar.

Thyme I like to grow the black thyme and the lemon thyme. They like a sunny position and the plants should be grown 2 ft by 18 ins. Cut twice a year in late May and late August. The rows should last six years.

16 Simple ways with fruit

One can grow excellent fruit in the normal garden with the minimum of labour. Where the garden is tiny, you can have what are known as 'family trees' which produce three or four different varieties from branches on one main stem. The nurseryman grafts them purposely this way and this saves a lot of trouble.

Often varieties are self-sterile – that is, they need the male pollen of another 'special' variety planted close by in order to cause their blossoms to set. On the family tree this happens automatically for variety A will pollinate variety B, and variety B pollinates variety C and so on. Those who have difficulty in buying family trees locally may, of course, write to the author.

In bigger gardens, the pollination problems may be solved by planting the right varieties, keeping an eye on what is called the fertility chart. This can be found in the book *The Compost Fruit Grower* published by Pelham Books. Fortunately, there is not the same difficulty with soft fruits.

The fruits that may be grown in the normal garden can be divided into three main groups:

1 strawberries;

2 raspberries, redcurrants and blackcurrants, logan-berries, blackberries and gooseberries;

3 the top fruits like apples, pears and plums.

Don't bother about growing cherries, because the sweet varieties need definite pollinators and are much better grown on large trees, and the sour or Morello cherries may not really be for the man who is going to 'enjoy his garden'.

STRAWBERRIES

The ground where they are to be grown should be covered with compost or medium-grade sedge peat $\frac{1}{2}$ inch deep. This may be lightly forked in or rotovated in. Strawberries must be planted in July or August to have a chance of settling down before the winter. They will crop heavily in the following year – and for three years after that.

Be sure to buy the right plants. Obtain a good strain of Cambridge Favourite such as the Elite Clone. Other varieties that are worthwhile planting are Templar which is a vigorous variety bearing medium-sized fruits of excellent appearance and Crusader, an early, extremely vigorous heavy cropper with superb flavour. The fruit is solid and firm. (If you have any difficulties in getting the right plants let me know, enclosing a stamped addressed envelope, please.) Ask the nurseryman to deliver the strawberry plants not later than the end of August.

Plant them in rows 2 ft apart, allowing 18 ins between the plants. Make a big hole with a trowel so that the roots can be spread out evenly, and then plant so that the roots are really firm. Use the handle of the trowel to push the soil well down and on top of the roots once they are spread out in the hole. Make certain that the crown of the strawberry plant – the centre part with the little leaves on – is just at the soil surface.

After planting, apply powdery compost or sedge peat all over the ground in order to keep down weeds and prevent moisture from evaporating. Make another slight application in early June (if the worms have pulled some of it into the ground during the winter), so that when cropping takes place in the summer, there will be sufficient peat all over the soil to keep clean the ripening berries. After the mulching there is nothing else to do except to see that the runners strike properly and immediately into the mulch, after all the strawberries have been gathered. You will thus produce some young plants for planting out in July or early August the following season.

PLATE 9. Strawberries with a 1 inch mulch of compost grow very large because the roots are never disturbed.

The gardener aims at keeping up the supply of healthy plants year after year. The original bed can usually stay where planted for four years, but it is of course important to obtain really healthy virus-free plants the first year, plants which strike their roots early and well into the peat put down as a mulch. Every year at least one row of young runners should be planted so as to carry on the virus-free strain.

As viruses are carried to the plants by vectors and as the vectors in this case are aphids, it is necessary to kill any aphids that appear on the undersides of the leaves. To kill the aphids therefore spray with a Derris-Pyrethrum wash late in April. Give a second thorough spraying after all the fruit has been picked. Be sure to cover the under-surfaces of the leaves.

RASPBERRIES, GOOSEBERRIES, RED-CURRANTS, BLACKCURRANTS AND BLACKBERRIES

These are soft fruits that can be mulched with straw 1 ft deep or, if you prefer, with sedge peat 1 inch deep. This group includes raspberries, gooseberries, loganberries, blackberries and red- and blackcurrants. These fruits grow well on no digging methods. There is a half-acre plot at the Arkley Horticultural College that has not been dug, forked or hoed since its time of planting in 1963, and it has grown excellent soft fruits for ten years and more.

The straw or hay method Immediately after planting, cover all the ground (not just along the rows) with straw or hay. Any straw or hay will do, but it must be at least a foot deep. It smothers the weeds, creates the right kind of mulch and prevents the moisture from evaporating, and so there is no digging, forking or hoeing to do. When picking time comes it is lovely to be able to walk on straw and have absolutely clean shoes. At the same time the gardener knows that he is not doing the roots any harm at all.

PLATE 10. The raspberries grow 9 foot high at Arkley Manor. They are mulched with straw 1 foot deep.

Blackcurrants, gooseberries and cane fruits grow very well under this system. The roots come right up to the surface of the ground, and they are never disturbed. The worms' humus-making activities enrich the soil year after year with more and more organic matter. It helps if a fish or seaweed manure with a 6 per cent potash content is applied at 3 ozs to the square yard all over the hay or straw in the spring, and again immediately after fruit picking.

This second application is to encourage the production of plenty of good wood which will crop the following season. It is most important in the case of blackcurrants to cut out about one fifth of the old branches each year and so produce plenty of young wood. The blackcurrant bears on the young wood, and you should aim to encourage the production of lots of young growth each season. The uninitiated are always very surprised at the heavy crops that result at Arkley under this system.

In the case of raspberries, there is no need to tie each cane to a wire running from one end of the row to another. Simply nail a T-piece on each post, and run parallel wires in between, the first about 4 ft high and the next about 6 ft high. The canes are then grown in between the two parallel wires, which are about 1 ft apart. There is no tying in, the canes are just pushed in between the wires, and there they stay and crop.

Gooseberries also can be grown under the straw-mulch system. By this method the berries are a little later. I think this is because the soil is kept cool and therefore they do not come into growth so early. Raspberries, loganberries, blackberries and even blackcurrants are not affected in this way. But by all means adopt the mulching system for gooseberries if you do not mind the berries being a little late.

The grass system The soft fruits in this case are planted in what is virtually a lawn. The rows are 6 or 7 ft apart and the bushes 4 ft apart in the rows. In the case of raspberries the canes are 18 ins apart, and with blackberries and loganberries 10 ft apart.

Holes are dug in the grass for planting the bushes or canes and the turf at this point is put back upside down. This planting is usually done in October.

In the spring and summer the grass is kept mown with a rotary cutter, the idea being to allow the lawn clippings to pass back to the soil. If the grass close around the actual bushes and canes gets long, it is cut with the Tarpen long-handled grass cutter with its $\frac{1}{2}$ h.p. engine. This enables the gardener to cut the grass extremely quickly right up to the base of the black currant or gooseberry or even to the base of the canes. The soft fruit is fed with fish manure, as advised in the case of the straw method.

APPLES, PEARS, PLUMS AND PEACHES

Apples and pears Lastly we come to Group 3, which consists of apples, pears, plums and peaches. The simplest form of apple tree to have in a mini-work garden is a bush grown on a weak stock. Few people realize that apple trees do not grow on their own roots; the nurseryman grafts them on to special root systems known to horti-culturalists as 'stocks'. For most gardens and most trees the type 9 stock is best. This produces dwarfing trees which never grow too large, and they begin cropping almost immediately. It is certainly the most suitable stock for cordons and even for strong varieties grown as espaliers. The only fault to be found with this stock is that the roots are so shallow and fibrous that the trees are apt to blow or lean over; but this only occurs in exposed gardens and where the trees crop very heavily on one side. It is, of course, easy to keep the trees permanently staked.

Old-fashioned gardeners make the mistake of digging over the ground and adding lots of compost. Land for apple and pear trees does not need treating in this way. A hole may be dug out about 2 ft across and a few inches deep and in the bottom of this shallow hole the roots should be spread out evenly and firmly. If the soil is sandy, aim to plant 8 or 9 ins deep, but if the soil is heavy the roots need only be buried 4 ins deep.

Never bury what is called the 'union of the stock and the scion' – that is, the point at which the nurseryman has done the budding or grafting. If you do, the variety itself will send out roots, and the great value of having your tree grafted or budded on to the 'special stock' will be lost.

It probably is not worth while growing cooking apples at all. This idea may be a shock to some! Eating apples cook beautifully; in fact one of the best apple pies is made with Cox's Orange Pippins. It may seem a shame to use a dessert variety for a pie, but if it tastes better in a pie than a Bramley, why not use a Cox – if there are plenty of this variety about? The mini-work gardener plans to have only dessert varieties that are useful to grow. I suggest Tydeman's Early Worcester, Worcester, Laxton's Exquisite, Fortune, Ellison's Orange, Cox's Orange Pippin and Laxton's Superb. These should give you a successional crop throughout the season. The Cox's Pippin is not too easy to grow, but it is mentioned because it is so delicious.

Plant as early as possible, preferably in November. In February cut back most of the 'end growths' or leaders (the lengths of one year old wood at the ends of the branches) by about half with a sharp knife or secateurs to just above a bud, but do not prune the side growths or laterals. In April or early May put a mulch around each tree of sedge peat, well-rotted compost or spent hops, to a depth of 2 ins and as far as the branches spread. The idea is to save any further cultivation and to allow the tree to grow naturally.

In a small garden most people want as many trees as possible, with a minimum of pruning. The trees on the Type 9 stock will not grow very large, nor do they need to be pruned hard. To be safe, plant them 12 ft apart, with about 9 to 10 ft between rows.

For the first two years the ground can be covered with straw to smother the weeds as in the case of the soft fruit. After that, the land can be sown with a grass mixture. An excellent one consists of eight parts Timothy S.50, three parts Red Fescue S.59 two parts white clover S.100 and one part wild white clover S.194. Sow this mixture at $\frac{1}{2}$ oz to the square yard, either in late March or late July. By grassing down in between the trees the weeds are of course kept down and the little orchard can be managed with the minimum of labour.

The following year cut the grass nine or ten times during the season with the mower blades set high and no grass-box. The grass clippings should be allowed to go back into the ground, where they will rot and be incorporated by worms. In January a fish manure, similar to that used in other parts of the garden, may be applied at 3 ozs to the square yard over the land. Allow it to wash in gradually.

Pears Most varieties of pears are self-sterile, so pollinators are very important. There are, however, a few varieties that are self-fertile; the best of these are Conference, Durondeau and Williams Bon Chrétien.

Plums Plums are also suitable for the minimum-work gardener. It is best to buy two year old bush trees, the most popular plum for the small garden being the Victoria, which is self-fertile. There are others that could be included because of self-fertility: a good cooker called Czar, and the dessert varieties, Denniston's Superb, Early Transparent Gage and Early Laxton. Plums do not do so well on grass as apples, and it is a good plan to give a little extra fish fertilizer to the plum trees, say in two applications, one in June and the other in September, each 3 ozs to the square yard. Incidentally, it pays to do all the plum pruning in the summer, because plums are susceptible to silver-leaf disease. When pruning is done in the summer months, this disease cannot attack through the wounds.

Peaches It may be worth while planting one bush peach. The variety Peregrine is easy to manage. Buy a three year old tree and plant in late October or early November. Prune in April when the trees are in leaf, cutting out the old hard wood to encourage the young growths on which the fruits are borne. Aim to keep the centre of the bush open, and try to keep the outside of it ball-shaped.

As the growths bear their fruit they tend to droop, and eventually the trees will get what is called a 'flattish' head. Do not allow the tree to overcrop: thin the fruits out when they are about the size of a walnut so that they are a hand's width apart.

PILLAR TREES

In our mini-work garden at Arkley Manor we have planted pillar trees. These are like single-stemmed cordons which grow upright to a height of, say, 10 ft. The trees are

planted 10 ft apart between the rows and 6 ft apart in
the rows. The main upright stem of a pillar tree is the
'framework' from which radiate the side branches on
which the apples and pears are borne. The pillar trees are
grown in a grass lawn which is kept cut regularly by a
rotary cutter. Once again the grass mowings are allowed
to lie where they fall so the soil is not robbed of organic
matter in any way.

The trees are planted in grass from the beginning and
are fed as advised for soft fruits. Use the Tarpen long-
handled grasscutter to cut the grass immediately around
the base of the trees where the rotary mower cannot work.

17 Mechanical aids for the garden

'It's no good trying to have a mini-work garden, it costs you the earth!', was an unfair criticism some time ago of Arkley Manor. You might as well say: 'It's no good trying to have a modern kitchen because you would be broke financially before it is finished!' It is only right and proper that garden and cookery advisers should be in a position to put people wise as to how time and labour can be saved by means of mechanical appliances. Some older folk reading this book will remember when the first vacuum cleaners came into vogue. At that time the debate centred around whether the actual vacuum cleaning was as good as the old-fashioned brushing by hand; then, when the old-fashioned conservatism had been beaten down, the question always was: could a vacuum cleaner possibly be afforded?

Today the demands of modern life are such that almost from the day a couple sets up home, they expect to have a washing machine, spin-dryer, and a refrigerator. Mechanical aids can take the arduousness out of gardening as well as housework. Don't let anyone say that new gardening schemes are too expensive, for remember that if Mr A. prefers, for the sake of exercise, to push a mower and to move the lawn mowings from the lawn by hand to the compost heap, then he must be allowed to do so. But then if he says: 'Please tell me how I can cut my lawn in an hour instead of taking up the whole evening doing it', the answer must be expressed in common currency whether this means an out-and-out expense, or whether it means a few pounds down and the rest paid on the 'never-never' basis.

In this chapter, therefore, will be found details of some of the implements that the author has found ideal for the

PLATE 11. The Auto Culto Rotary Cultivator saves any digging in the vegetable garden.

minimum-work garden, and a summary of what has previously been included under other headings.

Digging, forking and hoeing The minimum-work gardener does any cultivation that is absolutely necessary by means of a rotary cultivator such as the Rolo recommended in the previous chapter. In heavy soils, it is best used in the spring and in the case of sandy soils, in autumn. Hoeing between the rows is done by the same machine with the blades set very shallowly, but the rows have to be so planned that the machine can work down perfectly and easily between them.

Remember that in the case of rose beds, shrubberies and any other part of the flower garden sedge peat used as a mulch 1 inch deep means that no hoeing is necessary for there are no weeds. No digging is needed either in the normal way. A hole is made for the roots of the rose or shrub and the firm planting is done. Then follows the top dressing of peat.

PLATE 12. The Tarpen Cultivator works excellently between rows of plants. Note that it has the same engine and handle as the grass cutter and that the parts are therefore interchangeable.

Seed sowing When seeds have to be sown in long lines the Excel Hand Mechanical Sower may be used. It works as well with flower seeds as it does with vegetable seeds. It is a simple matter to move the disc so as to arrange that seeds are sown at given intervals. It comes from Russels, The Works, Kirbymoorside, York.

When seeds have to be sown broadcast, as for a lawn, then it is possible to use a machine like the Sisis, which consists of a long, V-shaped container under which runs a specially devised roller. The rubber-tyred wheels on either side of the machine operate the roller, so, as the seed sower is pushed forward, the seeds are deposited evenly all over the ground.

Organic fertilizer distribution To apply a fish or sea-weed manure evenly by hand on a lawn takes practice and it isn't every minimum-work gardener who has time to bring even fertilizer distribution to perfection. Use the Sisis fertilizer distributor. Fill the container with the necessary plant foods and when the machine is pushed forward, the right quantity is dropped onto the lawn where it is needed.

Hedge trimming One of the most labour saving tools is the electric hedge cutter which can cut up to ten times faster than a man with hand shears. As very few people have the time to cut their hedges properly, an electric cutter can be indispensable. Really good professional gardeners are difficult to find, and even if a garden owner is lucky enough to get hold of a first-class man, he will expect a very high hourly wage today. An electric hedgecutter may therefore repay its initial cost in a very short time.

The Tarpen Engineering Co. Limited offer two machines, one for the larger garden and a smaller type for the suburban garden. The Super-trimmer consists of an 18 inch blade driven via worm and pinion gears by an electric motor. An exclusive overload clutch is fitted to protect the mechanism from any hidden obstruction which might be encountered.

For smaller gardens there is the Easycut which is fitted with a 15 inch blade which will cut growth up to $\frac{5}{8}$ inch in diameter, and the Swiftsure, with its 12 inch blade, which is ideal for the small hedge, cutting growth up to $\frac{1}{2}$ inch in diameter.

The reciprocating blade ensures the clean secateur cut approved by experts. The teeth on the stationary blade are $\frac{1}{4}$ inch larger than those of the reciprocating blade, thus minimizing the risk of accident and at the same time acting as a guide to bring the right growth between the cutters.

The front handle on the Super-trimmer is fitted in such a way as to allow the operator to choose any position which is most comfortable for his or her use, while on the others a carefully developed front handle ensures easy use and good balance. Special 4 inch extension handles are available for the Super-trimmer and Easycut if these are required. They can be fitted to the machine in a few seconds and are a great help when cutting the sides of a high hedge or across the top of a wide one.

These British hedge cutters are double insulated for added safety and by using modern materials these machines are light and easy to operate.

Hedges are not always in a convenient place with regard to the main electricity supply, but I have found that Tarpen hedgecutters can be operated from small portable electric generators. In small gardens where there is insufficient work to justify the purchase of a special generator, then the 12 volt models can be run from the battery-operated lawnmowers, 12 volt car batteries, or the special heavy duty battery manufactured for use with 12 volt power tools. From one and a half to three hours' use can be obtained from the battery before recharging is necessary.

The Cordless Wilkinson Electric Hedge Trimmer
This is excellent for hedges and for the larger shrubs. The machine consists of two 14 inch non-stick double edged blades. They are perfectly balanced and are

surprisingly light in weight. Like the grass shears the electrical power operating machinery lasts for about fifty minutes running time. It has a similar nickel-cadnum battery that can be recharged. It is, of course, cordless and so movement is not restricted. It has an excellent blade guard and so is safe to handle. It has a charger which is provided free when the tool is purchased.

The Grassmaster Most gardens of any size have areas of grass which can only be cut with a hook or hand shears. It is therefore useful to own a machine called the Grass-master, which is specially designed to cut grass in awkward conditions, as on steep banks, ditch sides, around shrubs and trees, or close up against walls and rockeries. These jobs can be done not only more quickly, but with a minimum of effort.

The Grassmaster has three different fittings: the Ski-cut, which enables the machine to be slid upwards and forwards, even over rough ground; the wheeled model, which makes the job as easy as pushing a carpet sweeper, (with this machine, a cranked blade can be fitted for cutting any ornamental type of grass as close as a lawn-mower); a verge cutting attachment is available also which will convert the Grassmaster into a most efficient grassmaster. This cuts as fast as the gardener can move along sideways, say at speeds of a mile of edge in an hour! Rather than fit a battery on to the machine itself (which of course limits the size and capacity of the battery) Tarpen offer a haversack battery which gives over one and a half hours' use. These machines are all available for mains use if preferred or for use from the mains via a transformer converting the mains supply to 110 volts.

Hoe Tiller There are a variety of other machines for the keen gardener and one of particular interest is the Hoe Tiller. This machine is designed for preparing a tilth in confined places, or for hoeing weeds out in rows. This particular machine can be operated by a special electric motor, or a small petrol motor which fits directly to it.

Power to the engine of the machine is transmitted to one of the tools by means of a flexible shaft. The work-head is simply clamped or screwed to the shaft so as to enable each tool to be replaced by another in a few seconds. In addition to the Hoe Tiller this form of power can operate on an 18 inch hedgecutter, rotary grass cutter, chainsaw and a rotary pruning saw.

A trimming shear Wilkinsons make an effective cord-less, electric convertible shear which is quite suitable for grass trimming jobs, i.e. trimming the edges of a lawn where it meets a wall or a concrete edging. It is lightweight and can be converted into an upright operated shear from a hand shear in about fifteen seconds. The steel is specially toughened and the shears themselves have 4 inch non-stick blades. It is powered by nickel cadnum power cells which provide power for the operation of the machine for about fifty minutes. I found it useful because there was no trailing cord to restrict movement. A charger is included in the price of the machine so the battery can be recharged at home at the end of the hour.

The garden sweeper There is nothing more boring than sweeping up leaves. There is however, an excellent sweeper which provides an automatic, easy, quick way of clearing debris at all seasons and defies the frolic of the gales and winds at the same time. The leaves are picked up and thrown into a wide grass-box. Also the fast revolv-ing brushes tend to improve root growth and improve the lawn texture. This machine is light and smooth to run, it folds up when not in use and has a long life.

An automatic garden line One of the nuisances of sowing seeds in straight rows is that one needs to put down a line first in order to ensure that the rows are really straight. The normal garden line consists of a piece of rope wrapped round two garden pegs. It takes time to put down and a longer time to roll up and put away.

The Bagshaw line takes all the work out of planting at the correct distance because there is never any tangled or knotted string and the line can be put down in a jiffy. The line is mounted on a spring-loaded drum and when it is pegged out it remains all the time under tension.

To rewind all you have to do is to pull out the peg at the far end, walk towards the drum and the line then rewinds itself automatically. The line is made of Terylene so it is rot-proof, weather-proof and washable and it is marked in alternate colours at 1 ft intervals. The drum is rust-proof.

Tying up plants The tying up of plants can be a boring, tiring operation, but fortunately there are two aids which save time and trouble.

1 *The Twist-It Tie*. This consists of a narrow piece of special green weatherproof paper down the centre of which is a malleable wire. It looks like dark green ribbon $\frac{1}{4}$ inch wide, and is cut by the manufacturers in convenient lengths of 4, 5 and 6 ins. The gardener may buy the Twist-It Ties by the thousands if he wishes and they are not expensive.

The tie is placed round the stem and support and the end is twisted with the finger and thumb. In a flash the stem is secured.

2 *The Handicut Twine Cutter*. Those who prefer using string for tying up shrubs, Cordons or Espalier trees can use the Handicut Twine Cutter. There is a hole in the base of the specially designed handle through which the twine or string passes. The ball of twine can then be kept in the pocket and when the tie has been made there is no searching for mislaid scissors or fumbling for pocket knives, for the little Handicut tool is available on the string.

It has at the functioning end a plastic 'mouth' into which the string is put and is cut automatically. The string passes through the body of the cutter so that the cutter doesn't hang from the string but slides up and down. It is therefore always handy and it makes all the difference to tying up when the use of string or twine is essential.

The Webb Battery Lawn Edge Trimmer Trimming
a lawn with long-handled shears is hard work. With the
Webb Lawn Edge Trimmer you do not have to stoop but
just pull the lawn trimmer along with one hand while it
trims your edges cleanly.

It has a tubular handle with a non-slip grip, and a safety
lock with an on/off switch. The large, adjustable pivot
roller helps keep close contact with the edge, and, being
mounted forward of the blade, enables the cutting depth
to be adjusted merely by raising or lowering the hand
whilst in use. The 7-in blade revolves at 5,000 r.p.m.
giving approximately 10,000 cuts per minute. There is
usually a special cutting blade safety guard which protects
the operator. A separate $1\frac{1}{2}$ amp. charger can recharge
the battery in 12–15 hours. This trimmer cuts for approximately 45 minutes, i.e. about 1200 yards of edges.

PLATE 14. The Wilkinson Sword trimming shear.

PLATE 13. The Allen Sweeper. This gathers up all the leaves with the minimum of work.

Tool cleaning Gardeners like to wipe an oily rag over the blades of the hand tools used in the garden in order to keep them clean and bright and to prevent them from rusting. Ordinary oil, however, does not prevent rust and so there have been great disappointments in consequence.

Gardeners have welcomed Lubrafelt made by Fountain Holdings Limited of Southampton. This is a 10 inch square piece of felt fitted with a conveniently sized handle. This slides into a metal container of a similar size, at the base of which there is a scraper for removing the mud from the blades of spades and hoes, etc.

The Lubrafelt is quickly wiped over the outside of the steel and the right amount of special oil is deposited. It is then replaced in its holder.

The oil with which the Lubrafelt is impregnated keeps rust at bay and this makes all the difference to the blades of the tools.

Edgings to borders Gardeners often wonder how to keep the soil of a bed from falling on to the path. Wooden lathes, bricks, and even special glazed tiles have all been used but these are unsuccessful both because of their high initial expense and because pests breed under them. The 'Plastic Strip' Lawn Edge can't rust, is flexible, and practically indestructible. It can easily be cut and there is no difficulty at all in bending it round to conform with the contours of a shaped bed. It has 'turned-over' edges so that it can be handled without risk of cutting fingers.

The Plastic Strip' lasts almost for ever, there are no cracks or crannies in it which pests and diseases may breed and it is very easy to put down. Furthermore, it is comparatively inexpensive. It can be used at the edge of lawns to stop the grass spreading into a bed.

Pelleted seeds Some seedsmen offer what are called pelleted seeds. This is a revolutionary seed development. Each seed is coated with a fungicide, insecticide and a soil conditioner rolled up into a ball. This little ball which looks like a small pill is far easier to sow than a tiny seed. The organic matter around the seed gives it a wonderful start and this makes it possible not to sow seeds by the sprinkling method but to put them in separately. Thus one carrot seed can be placed exactly where the carrot is to grow, and there is no thinning to do later.

This spaced out sowing with the pelleted seeds results in stronger seedlings and, in consequence, earlier and better crops. It helps guard against baby seedlings being attacked by diseases in the pre-emergence stage or ruined by soil pests the moment they come through the ground, and saves the gardener a great deal of worry, and the money which he might have to spend on spraying and dusting later on.

The Picka-Uppa saves time and energy Everything that goes onto the compost heap, or even onto the bonfire has to be loaded into a wheelbarrow and then has to be transferred to its final destination. For such an operation the use of two pieces of board are not intelligent or adequate.

The Picka-Uppa is designed both as a time-save and probably even more important, a back saver. Many gardeners suffer from backache brought about by unnecessary stooping.

The large $13\frac{3}{4} \times 9\frac{1}{4}$ inch clam-shaped blades of the Picka-Uppa will pick up and hold a worthwhile load of garden debris. The lower edges of the clam blades are formed so that their edges meet when only light loads are picked up. This enables them to pick up any residue of earth, and small stones, leaving the surface of the soil or path absolutely clear. The finger moulded handles and the length of the shafts are designed so that loading is virtually effortless.

The blades of the Picka-Uppa can even lift almost the entire contents of leaves out of a canvas bag into which they have been placed and then deposit them exactly where they are required. It can deal equally well with acorns or rose-prunings.

For composters the Picka-Uppa saves endless time collecting small piles of dung from fields, yards and paths.

The Post Hole Borer The Maulden Engineering Co. Flitwick, Bedfordshire, make a New Post-Hole Borer which cuts into the soil and forces a core of soil and stones, up to 3 ins diameter, into the centre of the curved unit. This cylinder of soil can then be lifted out and shaken free.

A clear cut hole can be made up to 3 ft in depth and 8 ins diameter in about one minute, depending on soil conditions. The gardener simply turns the Borer by its tubular handle which has hardened steel cutting blades which force the soil upwards as the Unit is turned until the container is full. The soil can then be lifted out of the hole and deposited where required.

This borer is robustly constructed and is fully guaranteed for one year. It is invaluable for forestry work and tree planting and is most useful for putting posts into the ground.

The Easy Planter The Maulden Engineering Company also make an Easi-Planter specially designed for the gardener. It is simple and yet extremely robust. It is used with foot pressure so as to cut a 6 inch diameter core of earth to any depth up to 8 ins. The curved blades are then lifted and the trip lever at the stem operated so as to allow the core of soil to fall to the ground. The result as seen is a nice even hole with plenty of room for plant roots to spread and without side wall compaction, which can delay root action and subsequent plant development.

This hand tool is supplied complete with a 3 ft long stem and a 'T' piece handle grip. The hardened steel semi-circular and hinged cutting blades of the Easi-Planter makes a planting hole in a few seconds. It also has a release lever. It operates quite well in stony soil.

18 Technology in the greenhouse

A few years ago no one would have dared to mention the greenhouse when dealing with minimum gardening. Any glasshouse was a bind – not only did it mean carrying cans of water so that the pot plants could be given their daily or twice-daily dose, but it also meant pushing open ventilators, stoking boilers, carting quantities of coke or anthracite about – the very type of work most people seem to hate after a day's work.

Electricity today has largely taken the drudgery out of greenhouse work, and because almost all gardeners who take their gardening job seriously cannot do without a greenhouse, it is wonderful to be able to 'marry' the supply of electricity to the needs of a greenhouse grower.

By installing the correct thermostat, not only can one heat electrically but it is possible to have almost complete automatic control in addition, and also minimize the over-all electricity costs. It is possible to water or spray automatically, control the opening and closing of the ventilators automatically – all of this, incidentally, by the bi-metal rod thermostatic control. The savings ensured by using this superior instrument are naturally the greatest where really high temperatures are being maintained.

ELECTRIC HEATING

The reader should consult the local Electricity Board or a firm that makes all the incidental instruments. There are tubular heaters which can be mounted on the floors or walls either singly or in multiple ranks. Extra lengths can be added later if it is thought necessary to boost the heating capacity of the house. The fittings should be in rust-proof alloy and the ends should be sealed in order to guarantee spray-proof joints.

The tubular hot water heater should supply a useful reserve of heat in its five or six gallons of hot water and the temperature is therefore maintained some time after the electricity has been automatically switched off. Humidity is automatically controlled by means of a simple adjustment on the ventilating 'leads'.

You have no worry about frost with the automatic electric heater. It switches itself on and off at whatever temperature it is desired to keep the greenhouse. You decide on the greenhouse temperature and the thermostat does the rest. There will be no more lugging fuel around, no more wicks to trim or lamps to clean, no more stoking at midnight or worry when you are away for the weekend.

AUTOMATIC VENTILATION

The automatic ventilator is known as the 'Ventmaster'. It ensures correct ventilation. It efficiently moves the ventilator in accordance with the changes of temperature inside and the weather conditions outside. Furthermore, the 'Ventmaster' contains its own power supply. There is no electricity to worry about, for the power unit consists of a cylinder containing a mineral substance which expands and contracts with the slightest change of temperature. A stainless-steel piston connected by a bell crank lever to the ventilator push-rod does the job. The rod will not rust away because the materials are rust-proof and non-ferrous.

The Autovent For the greenhouse which must be left unattended for more than a few hours, automatic ventilation is a necessity. Temperature conditions inside the house can vary so greatly and so quickly that the precious plants can be upset.

For the amateur, the simple Autovent is a relatively inexpensive system. This uses the movement of a piston caused by the expansion and contractions of a sensitive wax contained within a cylinder, to open and close a vent.

Very few greenhouses are designed with sufficient

vent area to avoid excessive internal temperatures in midsummer even with the vents wide open. This fact should be borne in mind when deciding how many of the vents in the greenhouse should be fitted with Autovents. If any choice *has* to be made, it is usually better to operate the roof vents automatically, and the side vents manually. The latter can then be left open 2 to 3 ins and convection will ensure adequate circulation and ventilation through the automatically operated roof vents.

Which type of Autovent should you use? Generally speaking, vents up to 18 ins square can be operated satisfactorily with side fixing units (units fitted to one side of the vent).

Ventilators wider than 18 ins should be operated by centre fixing Autovents which are attached to the middle of the vent bottom rail and cill bar. These units lift the vent centrally and hence avoid any tendency to twist. Their design allows the incorporation of a strong spring which effectively damps out vent movements caused by wind buffeting. This can be a problem in the case of greenhouses in exposed areas.

An Autovent can be set to start operating at any temperature between 60°F and 100°F. As the temperature increases the vent is opened wider. The actual maximum opening depends on the size and weight of the vent; the heavier the vent the smaller the opening.

Corrosion is often a serious problem with greenhouse equipment. The Autovent however employs stainless steel, brass, aluminium and nylon and thus great care is taken in the design to avoid electrolytic corrosion.

The Autovent manufacturers – Bayliss Precision Components Limited, Ashbourne, Derbyshire – will answer any queries with regard to the fixing of their product to ventilators.

The Autovent arrives from the maker with full instructions as to fitting. At *The Good Gardeners' Association* trial grounds one of these Autovents has been working perfectly for ten years.

AUTOMATIC WATERING

There are two ways of watering automatically. The first is used when tomatoes and chrysanthemums are either growing in the ground or in pots and then it is possible to make certain that each plant has its own little nozzle which is firmly attached to narrow rubber tubing. The tap is turned on and the water then trickles down the narrow rubber tubing very slowly and water is given to each plant automatically by means of the cleverly constructed little nozzle. The advantage of this scheme is that no water is wasted and each plant receives the exact amount it needs. The disadvantage is that it is necessary to have a special 'harness' made to fit the layout of all the plants in the house and each year the gardener has to plant exactly in accordance with the previous year's plan, in order to fit what is called the trickle irrigation scheme.

The second idea is the one known as the Watermatic. Special nozzles are provided on metal stems fixed right the way down the greenhouse to a main control pipe. From these standard stems special nozzles are fixed and from these water is sent out with power as a fine mist-like spray. Thus artificial rain is given in a very fine foglike form whenever it is desired, absolutely automatically. The duration of the watering period is adjustable by the mere turn of a knob and may be made to last from a few seconds to several minutes. The time between the watering periods is governed automatically by the drying conditions produced by the sun and movement of air. There is of course an adjustment provided by the manufacturers at the initial setting up.

The water passes through a filter and fills the evaporating chamber of the detector. The water level in this chamber rises slowly, eventually reaching what are called the tips of the detector probes. The duration of the watering period is determined by the adjustment of the drip feed, and the length of time between the watering periods is adjustable by means of an overflow valve. It sounds complicated but it is quite simple in practice.

Those who want to have special mist sprays on the staging of the greenhouse for pot plants may use flexible polythene piping finely punctured at intervals as and where necessary. A gate valve can be provided for adjusting the pressure to this flexible line on one side and spray jets on the other. This is a wonderful saving of time and labour for the lazy gardener.

SHADING THE GLASS

Experts make it quite clear that in mid-summer when the sun is blazing, it is necessary to whitewash the outside of the greenhouse to 'break up' the sun's rays and provide the necessary shade. This is a messy, tedious job. It has to be put on in summer and scraped off at the end of September because by this time the plants need all the sunshine possible.

Fortunately, today there are roller shades which give the plants protection against the scorching sun. These roller shades are made of green translucent P.V.C. sheeting which is attached to robust self-acting spring rollers supplied complete with brackets and screws. They are fitted to a ledge inside the greenhouse and can be extended down either side of the roof as required. They can easily be pulled down to the level of the staging where they remain fixed without any adjustment and at a touch they roll up instantaneously and automatically.

Automatic blinds Automatic sun blinds are excellent. They are made by Automatic Sun Blind Installations, 98 Rushes Road, Petersfield, Hants. I can strongly recommend them. They run up and down automatically; when the sun comes out they come down and when the sun goes in they roll up. They are fixed outside the house.

Shading with Vari-Shade A revolutionary shade coating that changes with the weather is now available called Vari-Shade. You paint it on the outside of the glass in the normal way and the great advantage is that it is white, giving complete protection from the sun's rays. when it is fine and yet it is perfectly clear when wetted by the rain.

There is thus no letting up or down of a blind by hand or even by automation. 330 cc's concentrate is sufficient to cover 100 square feet, I have discovered. Full instructions as to its use are given on the plastic container when bought. It is made by Clovis Lands Associates, Gaza Estate, Weald, Hildenborough, Kent.

DOUBLE GLAZING

The glass used in double-glass greenhouses is essentially very thin. This is necessary firstly so that a light framework can be used to carry it and secondly to provide high light transmission. Because the glass is thin, heat passes through it easily and the cost of fuel to maintain the necessary temperature is high.

How can insulation be achieved without serious reduction of light transmission? Double glazing (two panes of glass, spaced with a layer of still air confined between them), is a possible answer. Using double glazing with an air space of $\frac{3}{4}$ inch reduces the heat loss to one half of that with single glass. Since the heat is retained, less make-up heat is required and less fuel has to be burned and so a smaller heating plant can be used.

There is thus a saving on both initial capital cost and running costs to set off against the increased cost of a double-glazed house as compared with a single-glazed one. Actually, one, two or three years are required to show a progressive gain. It is true that using two panes of glass does reduce the light transmission slightly (from eighty five to about seventy five per cent) but for the domestic grower this is not of great significance. Starting with a standard unit of 10 ft 6 inch by 8 ft additional extensions made up of 2 ft 6 inch units can be added when required.

OTHER MINI-WORK IDEAS

Sufficient has been said to show it is possible to have a greenhouse in which there is hardly any work. As a matter of fact it is better to have a cedar greenhouse because then there is no painting to be done.

The gardener should standardize the composts or soil mixtures he uses for the plants by buying a no-soil compost. This compost is suitable for any or all plants that are usually grown in greenhouses in this country. In the bags in which the compost is supplied is a special plastic bag containing the necessary plant foods. Instructions are given how much of these ready plant foods have to be mixed with the compost for the particular type of plant. Thus the main part of the compost is standardized and by the use of additives it can be made suitable for any crop. The Alex Peat Company of Burnham-on-Sea, Somerset, provides a booklet giving complete instructions.

If plastic pots are used throughout, then there are the minimum of breakages. The pots do not have to be scrubbed, because they remain naturally clean. Much less watering is needed as there is hardly any loss of moisture day by day. In the case of plastic pots there is no transpiration through the sides of the pot. Clay pots break easily, plastic pots do not. The outsides of clay pots often become covered with green slime and moss but this never happens with plastic pots.

Converting a coke boiler to oil It is possible to convert a hot water boiler heated by anthracite or coke to oil. This is extremely simple if the new Phillips Burner is used which fits into the fire-box without any difficulty at all. This conversion can be done by Messrs. H. E. Phillips Ltd. of King William Street, Coventry, Warwickshire. The heating of the greenhouse is absolutely automatic. There is no stoking, no carting of coke, no removal of ashes, no bother at all.

Lytag One of the problems of putting gravel or cinders on to staging is that after a time it becomes covered with moss and lichen. Ashes easily get sodden and so prevent perfect drainage. Lytag however is ideal, because it remains clean and never gets sodden. It looks like little grey pebbles and is very light in weight. It is obtainable from Laings of Edgware.

THE LIGHT METER AND LIGHT ENERGY

Much has been said and written about the desirability of automation in the greenhouses. How far a keen greenhouse owner should go in installing automatic equipment is a decision he must make in the light of his particular circumstances, and of his pocket!

The application of just the right amount of water, at the right time, makes all the difference between growing good or poor plants. Inside the protection of a greenhouse the most prominent factor influencing the need for water is the amount of light-energy which a plant receives. This can be measured by means of an integrating light-meter, so called because it continuously sums, or integrates, the amount of light falling on it. By using such an instrument the gardener knows just when and how much water to use. This by itself, although not completely automated, will correct at least one of the important operations in the growing of plants. It will be readily appreciated that this can be a vital, though short, step to automatic watering for using a special counting mechanism. The electronic experts have produced an inexpensive apparatus which ensures that water is applied from above just when it is needed.

Because the majority of plants demand a greater control of day temperatures than night temperatures, there must be a close relationship between the optimum day temperature and the light which is available at the time. It is not possible to maintain the optimum day temperature in a greenhouse by the normal method of setting the ventilators, unless the owner is there personally to control it. Many people today use light-meters in order to set their cameras, for the best results. The plan now is to do this for greenhouse plants. The instrument which can be used for irrigation control can also be used to provide the information upon which to control the day temperatures – and this also on an automatic basis.

For the amateur, the ventilator is invariably the means used for controlling day temperatures because round-the-clock heating is regarded as expensive, thus what extra heat is given is applied during the night. The little Ventilator-Openers, which resemble a bicycle pump, do operate by the heat of the sun. No greenhouse, therefore, should be without some form of automatic ventilation.

Having arranged automatic watering and automatic ventilation the garden owner is free to go away from home, not only just for a weekend, but even for a normal holiday.

The Aquafeed Moisture Matting The moisture bench principle saves endless watering and provides a good source of moisture which plants may draw on naturally by capillary action.

Sheer cost now compels amateurs to look for something which is light in construction and so can be used on ordinary greenhouse benches and further, which may be cleaned without the necessary labour associated with sand or gravel.

The Aquafeed Moistured Matting is fifty times lighter than sand. It has a high water retention, i.e. approximately one gallon per square yard. This is evenly distributed throughout the material along with a liquid feed, if necessary. Plants take up the moisture and plant food Aquafeed as they require it and all dangerous overwatering is eliminated. It is possible also to regulate the amount of water available in the moisture matting so that high moisture crops like lettuce etc. can be catered for as well as for plants like succulents which need little moisture.

Setting up the moisture bench is as easy as rolling out

the Moisture Matting onto a reasonably level surface. If you need a moisture bench in the early spring perhaps, and you wish to remove it in the early summer to make way for tomatoes, you can do so in a few minutes.

The cleaning of Moisture Matting is an easy task. It is a synthetic fibre and thus dirt gets *on* it but not *in* it. Simply wash and rinse! – This apparatus can be obtained from Amberol Limited, Railway Wharf, Derby Road, Belper, Derby DE5 1UX.

19 Weed killers

Weeds have been a problem since man was turned out of the Garden of Eden. The Bible makes this quite clear: 'Cursed is the ground for thy sake, in sorrow shalt thou eat of it all the days of thy life. Thorns and thistles shall it bring forth to thee!' (Genesis III, 16, 18)

A weed is a plant growing where it isn't wanted. A sweet-pea poking out of the middle of a row of carrots is a weed. A cauliflower trying to grow in the midst of a bed of Sweet Williams is a weed. The gardener therefore aims at having ground in which he can grow all the plants that he wants to produce, without any competition from thistles, nettles, groundsel, chickweed, bindweed and so on.

Not only do weeds take up moisture and foods which the plants ought to have but by their nature they grow very vigorously and tend to smother the cultivated plants and ruin them. The reason vegetables are grown in rows is because this leaves room for hoeing between them. *If* herbicides could be used so as to control all the weeds (and these are applied before seed sowing), then it might not be necessary (in future) to grow plants in rows at all. Seeds could be sown broadcast all over the land available and only those particular vegetable seeds would germinate and grow, and the eventual crop easily harvested at the end of the season. Herbicides however, discourage the work of the beneficial bacteria in the soil and so the author never uses them.

The pre-emergence weed-killer S.E.2 may be used to destroy weeds *before* the crops germinate. It is applied as a spray three to ten days after sowing and will destroy all weed seedlings so that no fresh ones will appear for three to four weeks. Thus the beds are left free from weeds over this period which gives the crops a very good start before there is any competition. It is possible to treat 200 square yards with S.E.2 for less than a pound.

Once again, the author wouldn't use a pre-emergence weed killer because of the danger of damage to the living beneficial soil bacteria.

For very coarse weeds

Gardeners sometimes take over plots of uncultivated or waste land where there are brambles, horse-radish or possibly tree stumps to cope with. It is therefore necessary to have a very strong hormone which will get rid of the lot without any difficulty at all. It must be a product which doesn't affect soil fertility or grass. It should be harmless to all human beings and animals and it must be deadly to all coarse weeds. The answer is a new powerful product, S.B.K. which contains the hormone 2,3,5-T.

Tree stumps This S.B.K. can be used at any time of the year. If there are old trunks of trees to get rid of, it is necessary to bore a few holes in the trunk, fill them up with undiluted S.B.K.: the hormone then gets to work and eats away the tree until, after a period of time, there is nothing left. Where there are quantities of strong weeds like thistles, nettles, bindweed and brambles, it is possible to treat a 500 square yard area for about 60p or 75p.

Weeds on a lawn

There are hormone selective weed-killers which can be used safely even on the finest grasses without fear of doing harm. They are usually of the M.C.P.A. type or may be a weaker solution of 2,4,5-T. They may be used to kill daisies, yarrow, buttercup and dandelions. These hormone weed-killers are diluted, watered all over the lawn and allowed to work naturally.

The hormones take a fair time to show their effect, but gradually the leaves of the weeds twist and curl and strangle themselves before dying. Some weeds like plantains and daisies are eradicated by one application at the normal rate; others, such as dandelions and creeping buttercup are usually eradicated by two applications at the normal rate.

Unfortunately, M.C.P.A. and 2,4-D are not really effective against such weeds as pearlwort, yarrow and clover: for these, use Fenoprop to control the first two and Mecoprop to control and kill clover.

Some hormone weed-killers sold by firms contain both Fenoprop and 2,4-D. These should be applied evenly all over the lawn, preferably during May and June. They are best applied by a watering can kept especially for the purpose.

There is one serious weed that is not controlled by hormones; this is moss. For this it is advisable to use a mercury moss eradicant at any time of the year at 4 ozs to the square yard. This is designed to eliminate any subsequent crop of moss although it doesn't kill the immediate growth. Those who do not mind temporary disfigurement may use an immediate mercury moss killer.

There is also a combined weed-killer and moss-killer which may be applied at the rate of 4 ozs to the square yard at any time between the early spring and late summer. It kills moss and weeds immediately and stimulates the growth of the grass at the same time.

Killing creeping grasses in cultivated land After eliminating all the normal weeds in a garden, we now face the problem of 'weed-grasses' like couch, (twitch and wick are other names for the same thing). Used at suitable concentrations the product Dowpon or Dalapon gives good control of couch grass and in fact would kill any member of the grass family. The author has used it successfully for wild oat, meadow grasses and bent grasses as well as on couch grass.

Dalapon should be applied in conditions that promote rapid growth: warm weather and moist soil. It acts best if put on after the soil has been forked and, if this can be done sufficiently early in the season, the disturbed couch 'roots' will re-grow. Then Dalapon should be applied just before the weed growth is 3 ins high.

Those who have bought a small Rotary Cultivator for

their vegetable garden will find this tool first class for disturbing the couch in the spring prior to the application of Dalapon. The substance is absorbed readily by both leaves and roots of plants and it is possible to get a ninety five per cent kill under these conditions.

If there is a certain amount of re-growth after treating, this is usually very feeble and may quickly be killed by normal applications. Readers who wish to get rid of couch on a neglected patch may use this method, and plant crops safely three weeks later.

Those who are organic gardeners and so do not like using such products should discourage couch by planting potatoes or tomatoes. Both are members of the *Solanaceae*. Such grass hates members of this family and disappear.

Weeds on paths After doing everything to minimize the crop of weeds in the cultivated parts of the garden, be sure to get rid of them altogether for at least a year by using a product containing Simazine. This is usually sold in Great Britain as Weedex and it can be applied at any time of the year. Its use in early spring or late autumn is advised, as this prevents weed emergence in the spring and summer. It is better to avoid applications during drought, frost or heavy rains.

Weedex kills weeds through their roots and then remains 'on guard' for a year or so, to kill any fresh weeds as they germinate.

Weedex is effective because it stays where it is needed – that is, on the top 4 ins of soil. It is practically insoluble in water so cannot be carried sideways or deeper into the soil by rain. This means that it can be applied safely on paths but will not spread out to kill plants nearby.

It is safe to handle and does not require any precaution whatsoever against fire as sodium chlorate does.

Annual weeds It has been discovered that there can easily be 250 million weed seeds in the top 3 or 4 ins of soil in a half-acre garden. Every time a man hoes he brings hundreds of weed seeds to the surface. These then germinate and in a few days the garden is a mass of annual weeds – groundsel, chickweed, fat hen, the lot.

The answer therefore is to leave the weed seeds where they are; that is below the surface. The weed seeds and baby seedlings that are growing on the surface must be smothered by covering the land with medium-grade sedge peat put on 1 inch deep.

It is this layer of organic matter (which could be your own powdery compost made in your own garden to save buying the peat) which will prevent any weeds from growing in future and which incidentally will keep the moisture in the soil.

BIOLOGICAL CONTROL

At the moment *The Good Gardeners' Association* are making trials in their experimental gardens at Arkley Manor. The planting of *Tagetes minuta* for instance does drive away convolvulus! It may also have an effect on other weeds like Ground Elder.

Any member of the *Solonaceae* family will drive away couch grass – particularly useful are tomato and potato. Moles may be kept at bay by planting Caper Spurge. The disease 'Leaf Curl' on peaches may be prevented by planting garlic cloves around the tree.

The experiments continue.

THE GOOD GARDENERS' ASSOCIATION

Throughout this book, mention has been made of *The Good Gardeners' Association* and of its headquarters, Arkley Manor.

Any reader may join the Association and visit the 8 acres of demonstration gardens at almost any time – except on Sundays. Members, called Fellows, get free advice by letter or telephone, as well as receiving bi-monthly bulletins. Demonstrations and lectures are arranged in different parts of the country and there are also branches overseas. For further details, write to the Association at Arkley Manor, Arkley, near Barnet, Hertfordshire.

Index

Page numbers in italics refer to illustrations

158

Shrubs and trees, 53–61: deciduous, 55, 64; electric hedge trimmer for, 132–3; evergreens, 54, 64, 69; hedge, 62–7; list of, 58–61; mulching, 55, 57, 129; planting, 53, 54–5, 57; preparation, 55; in wild garden (Henry VIII), 68–9

Sisis fertilizer distributor, 131

Sisis seed-sowing machine, 131

Sitwell, Sacheverell, 94

Smother plants/border, 47–52: list of suitable plants, 50–2; mulching 48, 50; planting, 49–50; preparation, 47–8; watering, 50

Snowdrops, 55, 71

Sodium chlorate, dry powdered (weed-killer), 47–8

Soil(s): of flower beds, 40; for heather garden, 82–3; humus content, 1; layer of compost or peat on top, 2, 15–16; lime, 70, 82, 94, 95; natural feeding of, 8–16; and natural return of organic matter to, 6–7; for primula border, 45; for roses, 73–4; treading, 48, 57, 63

Sorrel, 21, 116

Spinach, 106

Spin Trim, 28

Staking, 29–30, 42, 57, 63, 97

'Station' sowing method, 108, 109

Stitt, Col J. H., 45

Strawberries, 118, 119–21

Sweet-peas, 8, 9, 151

Swiftsure, 132

Tarpen Cultivator, *130*

Tarpen Grassmaster, 133

Tarpen Hedge Trimmers, 62, 131–2

Tarpen long-handled grass cutter, *21*, 123, 127

Tarragon, 116–17

Thistles, 31, 40, 48, 151, 152

Thyme, 117

Tibetan poppies, 55

Tomatoes, 4, 9, 107, 112, 144, 154, 155

Tool cleaning, 138

Top dressing *see* Mulch

Trevondan, Mrs Warwick, 24

Trickle irrigation scheme, 4, 144

Tulip silvestris (woodland tulip), 71

Turnips, 106

Twist-It Tie, 135

Tying-up plants, 135

Urine, used as liquid manure, 10

Valerian, 71

Vari-Shade, 145–6

Vegetables, 4–5, 103–13; mulching, 103, 104–7; no fruit trees in, 4–5; rotary cultivator for, 103, 104, 129, 153–4; saving labour with different types of, 108–12; sowing seeds, 103–4, 105; 107–8; 'station sowing', 108, 109; weed control, 103; without digging, 104–7

Ventmaster, 142

Viburnumtinus, 53

Vincas (periwinkle), 49

Violet, dog-toothed, 71

Wallflowers, 2, 29

Watering, 50, 95; Aquafeed Moisture Matting, 149–50; in greenhouse, 144–5, 148, 149; trickle irrigation scheme, 4, 144; Watermatic system, 144–5

Watermatic, 144–5

Webb Battery Lawn Edge Trimmer, 136

Weedex, 154

Weeds, weed-control, 151–5: in Alpine scree, 100; annual, 154–5; biological control, 155; creeping grasses, killing of, 153–4; eliminating tree stumps, 152; in flower beds, 40–1, 46, 47–8, 50; getting rid of perennial, xi, 31, 40–1, 48, 55, 73–4; hormone weed-killers, 17, 20–2, 40, 41, 47, 48, 73–4, 152–3; killing coarse weeds, 152; in lawns, control of, 17, 19, 20–2, 152–3; moss-killer, 153; mulching method to avoid